# THE JOURNAL

## OF

# BELARUSIAN STUDIES

Volume 8, Number 1, 2016

I0449025

## CONTENTS

# THE JOURNAL OF BELARUSIAN STUDIES

Founded 1965

| | |
|---|---|
| *Editor:* | Yaraslau Kryvoi |
| *Copy Editor:* | Jeremy Coppock |
| *Editorial Support:* | Vadzim Smok, Maryja Kavalčuk |
| *Advisory Board:* | Arnold McMillin (United Kingdom), Jim Dingley (United Kingdom), Andrej Kotljarchuk (Sweden), Curt Woolheiser (USA), David Marples (Canada), Iryna Dubianetskaya (Belarus), Andrew Wilson (United Kingdom) |

*Note:*

Items for publication in the Journal are subject to a refereeing process. The Journal of Belarusian Studies is published by the Ostrogorski Centre in cooperation with the Anglo-Belarusian Society. The views expressed by individual authors are not necessarily those held by the Editorial Committee, the Anglo-Belarusian Society or the Ostrogorski Centre.

ISSN 2053-4906 (print)   ISSN 2053-4914 (online)

*All correspondence relating to editorial matters, books for review and submissions should be addressed to:*

The Editor
The Journal of Belarusian Studies
4, 52 Penn Road, London N7 9RE
United Kingdom
editor@belarusjournal.com
http://belarusjournal.com

# Editorial

The 2016 issue of the Journal largely resulted from a conference organised by the Ostrogorski Centre and the UCL School of Slavonic and Eastern European Studies in London in March 2016. The conference gathered around 20 scholars of Belarus from the United Kingdom, Germany, United States, Canada, Poland, and France. Three papers were selected for publication alongside the annual lecture on Belarusian Studies delivered by Professor Andrew Wilson.

In the issue's first article, Aleksandra Pomiecko of the University of Toronto writes about the bandit-partisans of West Belarus in the 1920s. She notes that the history of the Second World War has often overshadowed less well-known parts of Belarusian history, such as the anti-Bolshevik movements on the territory of Belarus. The article analyses portrayals of bandits in newspapers to understand local perceptions in Belarus. The bandit Ataman Mukha exemplifies the 'heroic' and 'cult-like' effect of bandit organisations, and his portrayal illuminates local sentiments and perceptions. Collectively, the article seeks to describe local sentiments towards this phenomenon in the borderland region, which has traditionally been viewed in historiography from the perspective of occupational forces.

Veronica Laputska of the Polish Academy of Sciences analyses Nazi war criminals in Belarusian internet media discourse, discussing the cases of Andrei (Anthony) Sawoniuk and Vladimir Katriuk. The author distinguished between state-owned, 'neutral', and oppositional media coverage of the two war criminals. The author concludes that Russian propaganda wields profound influence on the Belarusian mass-media. She notes that rather than coming up with their own explanations, Belarusian state mass-media often merely echo the Russian media. This differs from the approach of 'neutral' and opposition newspapers, which in the majority of cases try to remain objective or oppose the messages of the Russian mass-media.

Ina Shakhrai of Humboldt University in Berlin examines the reactions to Alexievich's 2015 Nobel Prize win in Belarus and Russia. She focuses on the interconnections between the common Soviet past of the countries and the spread of nationalist sentiments in the post-Soviet space following the Ukrainian crisis. She argues that Alexievich's dismissal of autocratic regimes, alongside her identity – encompassing Soviet, Russian, Belarusian and Ukrainian elements – prevents her from becoming a unifying figure in Belarus and Russia.

Professor Andrew Wilson of University College London looks at how Belarus has transitioned from a social contract to a security contract after the start of the crisis in Ukraine. He observes a triple shift since 2014 as Russia became more aggressive towards its neighbours and Lukashenka shifted in a more statist direction, followed by part of the old opposition. Belarus has not been invaded, but a sense of threat, and a desire to avoid conflict, has led to a certain closing of ranks. Professor Wilson notes that it would be much easier for Russia to impose their own man at the top rather than break the bonds between the leader and the elite, or between the leader and society.

Dźmitry Papko of Warsaw University reviews a new collection of texts by Valancin Akudovič, one of the most renowned Belarusian philosophers. According to the review, Akudovič proves that Belarusian language, history, and culture are less important to the process of constructing the nation's collective identity than the mere existence of the Belarusian state.

Peter Braga of the School of Slavonic and Eastern European Studies analyses three articles on Belarus-China relations and the commitment of the Belarusian authorities to a high-risk strategy to bring in Chinese investment. The Chairman of the Anglo-Belarusian Society Brian Bennett also gives an annual account of the most important activities of the Society.

YARASLAU KRYVOI

# Villains, Profiteers, and 'Robin Hoods': Banditry in the North-Eastern Regions of the Second Polish Republic in the 1920s

## BY

## ALEKSANDRA POMIECKO

By the end of 1923, the man known as Józef Mucha-Michalski, or Ataman Mucha, could boast a repertoire that included armed robbery, theft, and murder in addition to party crashing, helping the poor, and regular dining at the most exclusive restaurants in Wilno. One day he was narrowly escaping the police in Galicja, and the next day he was blackmailing local government officials in Oszmiana. His reputation of irritating state institutions and helping and terrorizing locals, all while publicly embarrassing local government officials spread throughout the north-eastern provinces of the Polish Second Republic.

Despite attempts by Polish authorities to track, find, and put an end to Mucha's trouble-making activity, he was never officially captured. The character of Mucha simultaneously juxtaposed the image of a villain, profiteer, and 'Robin Hood' through his actions, both real and alleged, and through his description by the state and local media. Even when reporting his more devious acts, the media resorted to comedy and humour, while vilifying the state. Furthermore, his popularity transcended national and generational gaps, while stories and legends of him lived on well beyond the 1920s.

Mucha can be added to the list of characters known as 'bandits', whose multiple personalities and representations continue to complicate categorization used by scholars. Nevertheless, his story – however real or fantastical- found a place and audience in the borderland region of eastern Poland. As such, studying myths and anecdotes, as reflections of society, is crucial for studying cases of banditry.[1]

The case of Mucha is but one example of a bandit figure who thrived in the post-First World War Period in the eastern territories of the Second Polish Republic. The signing of the Treaty of Riga in 1921 officially consolidated the borders between

---

[1] This article chooses to use the term 'banditism' as this was the official term relegated to particular acts committed in these territories under the Second Polish Republic. In doing so, it does not attempt to undermine groups that were more ideologically and politically motivated or organized.

the Soviet and Polish states. Subsequent wars between Lithuanians, Poles, and Ukrainians would fine-tune official demarcations by the mid 1920s. Nevertheless, the official, diplomatic negotiation of borders far from clarified the situation for people at the local level. A study by James Scott of the Zomia region in Southeast Asia offers an appropriate framework through which to better understand the situation on the ground. As Scott argues, the Zomia was an area that essentially operated as an enclave community. Inhabitants of the region had little regard for official rule and administration, interacting with official authorities only when necessary (Scott 2009, 329). Scott's exploration of the Zomia parallels that of the *kresy,* or borderland region. At the local level, every-day people were trying to survive in the newly-created Second Polish Republic, which suffered from a lack of rule of law in addition to a decaying economy. This left a vacuum for discontent by locals, who distant from both Moscow and Warsaw, increasingly lost trust in official authorities who seemed uninterested in helping.

The politically and economically unstable atmosphere following the First World War was fertile ground for bandit-related activities, as incompetent governmental forces failed to effectively track and penalize those guilty of such crimes. Bandit related crimes, which were categorized as theft, armed robbery, destruction of property, and murder, peaked between 1922 and 1923. Subsequently, the local opinion of state or occupying forces and institutions became increasingly negative, as reflected in the local press and Polish government reports, while bandits offered a source of comedy.

This article discusses the dissemination and prevalence of banditry from the early to mid-1920s in the north-eastern region of the Second Republic of Poland, primarily in the provinces of Wilno, Białystok, Nowogródek, and Polesie.[2] Collectively, individuals who chose the bandit-partisan life embody the historiographical foci that have enticed scholars studying the *kresy.* They frequently moved between borders, interacted with locals of various national and ethnic backgrounds, as well as with state institutions – whether it was the police, army, or civil administration. They were often former soldiers who experienced violence as a result of war, and frequently engaged in such acts during their raids. As such, this category of individual serves as a fulcrum for various crucial historiographical tropes; focusing on them provides a lens through which to better understand larger questions regarding the chronologies of war.

This article will firstly offer a historical background regarding the area in question as a means of contextualizing the later analytical portion. It will then move on to discuss the historiography of banditry in the borderland region, which

---

[2]   This article uses the terminology and spelling of locations as it officially appeared during the Second Polish Republic. Most of the subject area today is part of the Republic of Belarus, mainly in the Hrodna, Brest, and smaller portions of the Minsk and Viciebsk provinces.

has been largely overshadowed by partisan literature covering the Second World War in Belarus. This will be followed by a brief description focusing on proponents and critics of Eric Hobsbawm's analytical framework that has been utilized to study banditry the world over. Having examined the historical and theoretical background, the focus will shift to banditism, its relationship to the state, and bandits' identities. It will then highlight one infamous example, Ataman Mucha, as a case study of how locals perceived bandits. Using material from archives in Maladečna, Grodno, and Minsk, as well as local papers from the early 1920s taken from the Academy of Sciences Library in Minsk, this paper will use bandits as a lens to flesh out a perspective that can contribute to our understanding of this region. Furthermore, with a focus on the post-war period, it seeks to question the 'beginning' and 'ends' of war and bring attention to the nuances periodization may ignore.

## Historiography

Studies of the borderland region have focused on refugees, state-building efforts, and the re-emergence of nationalism, to name a few tropes within the historiography. Some scholars have used the term 'shatter-zones' to better examine the geopolitical dimensions of this region. More specifically, Omer Bartov and Eric Weitz suggest that because these borderlands are distantly situated from a central point of power, they become 'constructs of the political imaginary and products of ideological fantasies' (Bartov and Weitz 2013, 1-2). As such, the borderland region has been at the centre of studies of war and violence.[3] This focus has been used to tease out ethnic, national, and political repression, as governing or occupying states ostracized local residents. It has offered a top-bottom schematic through which to understand certain issues, particularly the relationship between the 'occupier' and the 'occupied'.

Scholarship and interpretative narratives of bandits and partisans have been largely coloured, if not tainted, by regimes that used such individuals as political tools. This forms part of a larger debate regarding the partisans of the Great Patriotic War, but the earlier interwar period receives less attention. Most of the scholarly information that does exist rests on the shoulders of a few Belarusian scholars, who mainly discuss the reaction of Soviet and Polish authorities to the dissemination of bandit-related activity. The other issue that garners attention, also by Belarusian scholars, is the general exacerbation of bandit-related activity after the failed Sluck Uprising in November 1920, discussed in a later section. In Belarusian archives, individuals active in the western regions of Belarus are categorized as Soviet partisans who were ideologically in tangent with the Bolsheviks.

---

[3] For examples of such literature, see: Alexander Prusin, *The Lands Between: Conflict in the East European Borderlands, 1870-1992*; Kate Brown, *A Biography of No Place*; J. Böhler, W. Borodziej, and J. von Puttkamer (eds), *Legacies of Violence: Eastern Europe's First World War;* Per Anders Rudling, *The Rise and Fall of Belarusian Nationalism 1906-1931.*

During the Soviet period, historians described them as schooled in communist ideology and always traveling or acting with a political agent present, who would teach them proper Bolshevik ideology to abide by (Poluian and Poluian 1962, 67). These 'partisans' are perceived to be 'bandits' in Polish sources. The same terminological swap occurs when individuals stray from the Bolshevik line and are then described as bandits by Soviet authorities. In her work, Valiancina Kuźmič proposes the term 'illegal armed formations' as a more appropriate way of categorizing these individuals, which is derived from a longer list of terminological labels including 'bandits', 'partisans', 'insurgents', and 'sabotage units or detachments' (Kuźmič 2009, 19-20).

## *Banditism* as an Analytical Framework

Endemic to the developing understanding and study of bandits is Eric Hobsbawm's work, *Primitive Rebels* (1959), and more pertinent here, *Bandits* (1969). The latter discusses *social bandits* and defines them as 'peasant outlaws whom the lord and state regard as criminals, but who remain within the peasant society, and are considered by their people as heroes, as champions, avengers, fighters for justice, perhaps even leaders of liberation, and in any case as men to be admired, helped and supported' (Hobsbawm 1981, 17).[4] Allen Isaacman underscores two important contributions of Hobsbawm's work to our understanding of bandits.

The first includes the synthesis of an analytical framework that can be used to delineate different individuals, who were historically labelled as 'criminals' by the state (Isaacman 1977, 2). Secondly, Hobsbawm's discussion stresses the universality of banditism, which has only been demonstrated by continuous multi-geographic studies that incorporate Hobsbawm's tenets. Nevertheless, as much as his definition offers some nuance in terminology, it avoids specificity, allowing social banditry to be a rather malleable analytical lens. Furthermore, since Hobsbawm's publication, scholars have demonstrated that figures perceived to be social bandits under the latter's definition were far from flat characters, but in fact complex individuals with conflicting repertoires and descriptions. As such, terms such as criminals, thugs, crooks, heroes, brigands, and hooligans continue to be murky and unclear.

In his work on the 19th century Lithuanian Bandit Tadas Blinda, Tomas Balkelis expands Hobsbawm's notion of 'national liberation bandits', in order to tease out how national myths were created and disseminated in peasant-based communities by patriotic elites, through their use of bandit stories. He further highlights that this

---

[4]  In his work, Hobsbawm focuses on three categories of social bandits: the *noble robber,* the *avengers,* and the *haiduk.* Furthermore, he focuses on non-urban settings and delineates social bandits from underworld gangs and from 'free booters'.

process was particularly prescient in 'peasant-based and non-dominant East European societies' as 'the process of nation-making followed the lines of social conflict' (Balkelis 2008, 114). The work is another example of a particular case drawing from a specific element of Hobsbawm's earlier work. In this case, the relationship between bandit narratives and national myth-making is highlighted. However, in the context of interwar northeastern Poland, where national-awareness was low, the correlation is not quite as strong. Illiteracy, and a lack of understanding of nationality or ethnicity, led many people to associate themselves with their local communities and, hence, saw themselves as 'locals', or *tutejszy* (Rudling 2015, 171).

Criticism of Hobsbawm's work has cautioned against his romanticizing of bandits and his use of popular folklore, myths, and ballads. Anton Blok discourages readers and researchers from glorifying social bandits. His work explores how such individuals were oftentimes self-serving and, as a whole, actually inhibited the solidification of peasantry as a class, because the bandit life offered an escape and opportunity for social advancement (Blok 1972, 496-497). This notion is accentuated by Peter Singelmann in his work on the *cangaceiro* in north-eastern Brazil. In addition to impeding the fortification of the peasantry as a strong and powerful class, Singelmann notes that the *cangaceiro* actually delineates itself as a category from social bandits because of its straddling relationship between the nobility and peasantry (Singelmann 1975, 59-83). Historians focusing on Latin America have pointed out one big flaw in Hobsbawm's work: the 'special relationship' between the peasant and bandit, which many claim is historically absent in this part of the world (Slatta 2004, 29). In fact, scholars point to the fact that bandits actually catered more to elite interests than they did to the peasants (Slatta 2004, 30).

The issue of sources is an interesting and important one. While scholars have been critical of Hobsbawm's utilization of non-archival or substantiated sources, the reality is that accurate biographical information on some of the most notorious bandits is murky, at best. Tomas Balkelis notes this in his discussion of the Lithuanian bandit Tadas Blinda when attempting to provide historical context for this individual's real life. Furthermore, even when government or official reports are available, they are often ridden with negative descriptions of the rebels attempting to 'strip them of political legitimacy, and reduce their popular support' (Slatta 2004, 27).

Any debate about bandits involves some sort of criticism of Hobsbawm's work or a utilization of the Hobsbawm-Blok paradigm, which allows scholars to tease out important elements from both and apply them to particular cases. Despite the continued debate and criticism of Hobsbawm's work, now published almost fifty years ago, his framework continues to be foundational for scholars working on this topic.

## Historical Context

To better explore the spread of banditry and such activity in the early 1920s, a historical context involving both war and policies of the Second Polish Republic is necessary. The experience of war, including the First World War as well as subsequent wars between Poles, Lithuanians, Ukrainians, and Bolsheviks, shaped the space through shifting borders and massive movements of people (whether voluntary or forced) including remnants of national or state armies and refugees. This historical context seeks to set the stage for better understanding post-war bandit activity. As such, it highlights elements that contributed to the later dissemination of banditism, by discussing movements of people, armed formations, and Polish rule over its eastern territories.

Both the German and Russian military occupations played a role in the mass relocation of civilians – whether voluntary or forced. The Russian army participated in these mass deportations, initially with alleged enemies, including Germans and Jews (Prusin 2010, 54). In the Spring of 1915, with the growing strength of the German and Austrian offensives, the Russians decided to retreat, practicing a scorched earth policy to limit potential material that could be used by the enemy. With this retreat came rumours of the atrocities that Germans would commit against locals who remained, prompting many to migrate eastward. Most of the evacuees were of Orthodox faith and lived in the regions of Grodno, Wilno, and Minsk. Exact figures of refugees are unclear, but the number varies between one and two million.[5]

By the fall of 1915, the war front moved toward the Dzvinsk-Pastavy-Baranavičy-Pinsk line as the Germans continued to push eastward, culminating in a concentration of about 2.5 million soldiers on both sides of the front line (Mironowicz 1999, 26). The regions of Wilno, Grodno, and Białystok, among others, became part of the German-governed region called *Ober Ost*. The German military occupation proved to be, in many ways, more open and equal than its predecessor. Newspapers and official decrees were published in national languages, as were identification cards. However, these cultural, educational, and linguistic opportunities were matched with heavy exploitation of local labour and resources, used to support the German army (Prusin 2010, 61). Under the Germans, a further 1,300,000 refugees were evacuated in 1917, from the Ober Ost region to Russia and Ukraine (Vesialkoŭski 1996, 91-97). As a result of these exploitive measures, resistance to the Germans crystallized. One manifestation of this process was an increase in guerrilla warfare, typically organized by Russians and locals in cooperation. The further deteriorating economic situation led to more desertions and a proliferation of armed groups. Some of these units became powerful and opted to raid and kill not only Germans, but locals as well (Prusin 2010, 62).

---

[5] Eugeniusz Mironowicz estimates the figure to be around one million, based on the difference in population numbers taken from population figures in Russia, which increased by one million between 1916 and 1918. Jury Vesialkoŭski opts for a number closer to two million.

Aside from desertions, movement of people, and the worsening economic situation, one incident that must be mentioned is the Sluck Uprising of November of 1920, which contributed to the further dissemination of bandit activity in the western Belarusian regions. Sluck played an important role in the history of Belarusian nationalism and Belarusian military formations. The region itself maintained the strongest awareness of Belarusian identity, which intensified during the 1917 revolution with the creation of a Belarusian National Committee.[6] Towards the end of the First World War, with the retreat of the Germans westwards, Sluck was occupied by both the Bolsheviks in December 1918 and later by the Poles in June 1919 (Vesialkoŭski 1996, 268). In October 1920, negotiations began between the Poles and Bolsheviks, leading to a demarcation line in Belarus. As a result, on 12 October 1920, the Sluck region became part of Bolshevik territory, sparking an anti-Bolshevik uprising.

A Sluck Brigade, organized into two regiments, was organized and the first armed outburst came on the 26 to 27 November 1920, concluding in a victory for Sluck. There were approximately four thousand participating armed soldiers, later joined by more Red Army deserters (Mironowicz 1996, 51). Despite the initial success and euphoria, the participants were only able to fend off the Bolsheviks for about a month, due to a diminished supply of materials and ammunition. Many of these soldiers fled to the West, hoping to seek help from the Poles, but were subsequently caught and imprisoned, as Polish authorities did not want to sour their peace negotiations with the Bolsheviks.[7] Those that remained in Sluck were arrested by the Bolsheviks, the majority of whom were sent to the Gulag where they did not survive. Still, there were those who escaped, both from the Poles and Bolsheviks, and continued to fight. Some joined smaller armed groups in the forests, one of these being the *Zialony Dub* group,[8] while others joined larger units, such as the Belarusian People's Republic anti-Polish organized armed formations under Vaclav Lastoŭski in Kaunas. These groups will be discussed in more detail later.

With the conclusion of the First World War came the collapse of three major empires, leaving a power vacuum in the borderland regions. As both German and Russian occupational forces retreated from the region, a space was created which was open and free, and in which 'multiple protagonists were able to make their own rules of warfare' (Prusin 2010, 73).

---

[6]   The Belarusian National Committee in Sluck preceded the official 25 March 1918 declaration of the Belarusian People's Republic in Minsk. Paviel Žaŭryd was the leader of the committee, which also maintained a newspaper called *Rodny Krai.*

[7]   The Sluck uprising participants, totaling approximately 1500 people, were held by Polish forces and subsequently sent to a prison in Daragusk and held there until May 1921.

[8]   *Zialony Dub* was an anti-Bolshevik armed group, composed of Red Army deserters, operating mainly in the Pinsk region. For more information, see: Nina Stužynskaja, *Bielaruś Miaciežnaja: z historyi ŭzbrojenaha antysavieckaha supracivu ŭ 1920-ja hh*, 2012.

## Polish Occupation Politics

At the conclusion of the Polish-Bolshevik War with the signing of the Treaty of Riga on 18 March 1921, the north-eastern region of the Second Republic of Poland (1919-1939) was organized into the Polish provinces (*województwa*) of Wilno, Białystok, Nowogródek, and Polesie.[9] These provinces were inhabited mostly by non-Poles and more specifically by Belarusians, Ukrainians, and Jews (Cichoracki 2012, 17). Despite the existence of a 1921 census, realistic population figures, particularly in the eastern provinces, are difficult to ascertain due to the fact that officials artificially elevated the number of Poles in the area to justify territorial inclusion into Poland (Żarnowski 1973, 372).[10] Despite this, one set of statistics found in Janusz Żarnowski's work based on the 1921 census offers some insight into the native languages spoken by the inhabitants.

In the Wilno province 60 percent claimed Polish as their mother tongue, in Nowogródek 53 percent of the population spoke Polish, in Białystok 67 percent, and in Polesie only 14 percent.[11] While linguistic inclinations and usage are not indicative of how people perceived their nationality, it still offers some sort of landscape for better understanding the diversity of the region. A less contentious data pool comes from a 1931 census, which gave a population figure of 31,916,000 for the entire republic, out of which Belarusians, Ukrainians, and Jews made up approximately 25 percent (Żarnowski 1973, 374).[12] While these figures are dated after this article's chronological focus, they offer a more reliable statistic, often used by scholars wanting to get a more accurate picture of the region's ethnic landscape.

Officially, the March 1921 constitution promised the sanctity of property, freedom, and life to all residents in the Second Polish Republic, irrespective of nationality, ethnicity, religion, or sex. Freedom of the press was also guaranteed, irrespective of language or nationality (Wróbel 2010, 132). In reality, however, Polish policies vis-à-vis its newly acquired eastern territories treated the region as a colonial entity. These policies of the Second Polish Republic would only compound already-existing struggles experienced by locals as a result of war. Abuses and exploitation of locals began prior to the official signing of the Treaty of Riga. Reports from Polish government and administrative officials repeatedly highlighted the abuses experienced by locals at the hands of Polish soldiers. A

---

[9] Officially, only Nowogródek, Polesie, Wilno (and Wołyn) were part of the eastern territories; however, parts of Białystok, especially in the Grodno and Suwałki counties, also recorded many cases of bandit-related activity.

[10] The 1921 census reported a total population of 25, 694,700 out of which approximately 15% were Ukrainian, 8% were Jews, 4% were Belarusians, and 0.1% were 'tutejszy'.

[11] The predominant number of those living in Polesie, 63 %, indicated they spoke 'tutejszy'.

[12] In addition to these categories in the acquired eastern provinces, according to the 1931 census there was an approximate one million 'Tutejszy' in the Polesie region. Other studies from Landau, Tomaszewski and Krysiński offer much smaller numbers for this category.

report by a government informant in November 1920 stated that not only Jews and Belarusians, but also Poles were very discouraged by Polish soldiers and some were even terrorized by them. The informant highlighted cases of theft, alcoholism, and 'wild behaviour' by Polish officers (Mironowicz 2007, 29). In another report from January 1921, a border control representative observed that locals were apathetic to both Bolshevik and Polish troops, who confiscated their milk, butter, cheese, meat, and bread. Many locals were even forced to join the army through kidnapping (Mironowicz 2007, 29).

The newly re-created Polish state suffered from a series of incapable coalition governments, unable to put together a reliable policy vis-à-vis the state's national minorities. The consistent drive focused on maintaining borders and assimilating Slavic minorities (Rudling 2015, 167). After the conclusion of the Polish-Bolshevik war, *polonization* efforts commenced in a more administrative way. The policy was an attempt to assimilate Poland's eastern minorities, primarily Belarusians and Ukrainians. One effect of this was the liquidation of non-Polish schools, as well as cultural and pedagogical institutes, and the confiscation of non-Polish press (Mironowicz 1999, 85).[13]

Land and power remained in the hands of wealthier Poles, as around 37 per cent of farmland in the north-eastern Polish provinces was owned by Polish landowners, and many Polish war veterans, or *osadnicy*, received land as compensation for their military service (Rudling 2015, 170). There was a shortage of basic goods which remained consistent during the war and was later exacerbated during Władysław Grabski's[14] economic reforms, which included strict savings, increased taxation, and the sale of state enterprises (Wróbel 2010, 139).[15] In the north-eastern provinces, this was compounded by an existing social structure, putting Polish elites at the top of the hierarchy. Scholars have indicated that most members of the Polish nobility, or *szlachta,* were not actually financially better off or wealthier than non-Poles. What differentiated this aristocratic class from others were historical roots in rank, culture, or class (Żarnowski 1973, 186-187).[16] Regardless of the economic realities of this class, to peasants and non-Poles they were seen negatively and blamed for exploiting locals.

---

[13] *Polonization* practices were not part of an official parliamentary process, but a systematic effort enacted by the Ministry of Internal Affairs, Ministry of Foreign Affairs, Ministry of Military Affairs,

[14] Władysław Grabski (1874-1938): Prime Minister of Poland in 1920 and from 1923 to 1925. He is associated with the *polonization* drive, along with others such as Leopold Skulski, Władysław Studnicki, and Grabski's brother, Stanisław Grabski who was the minister of religion and education in 1923 and 1925-1926.

[15] Grabski's policies were implemented in an already-existing unstable political and economic system. In 1920, there were six different currencies circulating in Poland, as well as nine varying fiscal systems.

[16] Many years prior to the First World War, there was actually a natural process of de-*polonization* amongst this class and many had been orthodox or even Tatars. The years immediately preceding the war witnessed a re-*polonization* process.

One of the reasons for the intensification of assimilation efforts by Polish officials was fear that Soviet Russia would attempt to utilize the minorities in the eastern territories against Poland. This fear was shared by Stanisław Downarowicz, the provincial governor of Polesie. His proposed assimilation plan highlighted the fact that most of the minorities were peasants – passive, poorly-educated and not unified by a strong political awareness. Therefore, it was crucial to separate these national groups – namely Belarusians from Ukrainians- in order to integrate them better. Furthermore, what was required from the Polish government was not political support, but rather financial and economic assistance (Mironowicz 2007, 36-37).

The combination of war-time experiences and the first years of *polonization* efforts by the Second Polish Republic set the stage for banditry. Years of exploitative and abusive occupation under German, Russian, and now Polish rule conditioned locals to distrust government and administrative officials. Nestled along the borders between Lithuania, Poland, and Soviet Russia, this peripheral region maintained a safe distance from larger centres of power such as Warsaw and Moscow and were more concerned with their local communities and livelihoods. Attempts to control, tax, and dictate a particular way of life were seen as a threat and would continue to cause friction between locals in the borderland region and the state.

## Order in the Wild East: Banditism as a State Weapon

Banditism proved to be a serious issue for both Polish and Soviet authorities. With murky borders, the aftermath of several wars, and lack of economic and political stability, movement of people between frontiers became much more fluid, despite the signing of the Treaty of Riga (Kowalski 1998, 139). Between 1919 and 1924, around 700,000 former refugees returned to the newly created Second Polish Republic (Poluian and Poluian 1962, 41). According to other historians, figures may have been higher, constituting between 25 and 35 percent of the population in the newly acquired eastern territories of the Second Polish Republic (Sorokin 1970, 17). Between 1922 and 1923, the regions of Nowogródek, Polesie, and Wilno witnessed anywhere from 650 to 1,400 bandit-related crimes (Śleszyński 2005, 41-42 and Paciorkowski, May 2014).

With swamps, thick forests, and lakes covering much of the north-eastern territories of interwar Poland, the area was highly conducive to bandit-related activity, where victims and perpetrators could easily hide and escape from official anti-bandit units or police forces. Heightened cases of banditry in the borderland region often occurred tangentially with wars or during periods of tensions between Poland and its neighbouring states – Lithuania and Soviet Russia – and continued after war was officially over. There were two geographical points in this region from which bandit activity emanated in the immediate post-First World War period. The Polish-Lithuanian War (1919-1920) inspired Belarusian nationalists to organize Belarusian armed formations and organize operations.

Vaclaŭ Lastoŭski himself received 40 million marks as a loan in order to organize anti-Polish operations (Śleszyński 2005, 10). These units were to officially represent the Belarusian People's Republic (BNR), but realistically were subordinate to the Lithuanian Army. Four armed subgroups were organized in the counties of Wilno, Oszmiana, Brasław, and Grodno. One of the most feared of these armed groups was led by Jan Hryciuk (pseud. 'Chort') who, during one operation on the night of 27 April 1923, murdered two police officers in the town of Kleszczele, along with the owner of the local restaurant and the latter's mother (Śleszyński 2005, 12).

Another infamous fighter in this area was Viačaslaŭ Razumovič, otherwise known as Ataman Chmara. He was the son of a priest in Grodno, had formerly fought in the tsarist army, and later received permission to be a trader and bring goods from central to eastern Poland. According to his memoirs, Razumovič was officially part of a Belarusian insurgent group, but was not convinced by Belarusian national aspirations. Rather, it seems that he wanted to use Belarusian organizations as a platform against Polish occupational forces, whether or not units were uniformly 'Belarusian' in identity (Nacyjanaĺny Archiŭ Respubliki Bielaruś f. 242п op. 2 d. 442, 13).

Officially, the BNR boasted around 12,000 Belarusian men fighting in partisan units or involved in covert activity. Most of these were peasants, with little to no experience in war and without a strong political orientation. Politicized individuals fighting for an independent Belarus were few and far between (Śleszyński 2005, 13). After the invasion of Wilno by Polish troops and following the signing of a treaty with Lithuania which diplomatically demarcated a border on 15 March 1923, the Lithuanians officially pulled back their support for Belarusian, anti-Polish operations (Śleszyński 2005, 14).

The second geographical arena for banditry was along the Polish-Soviet border, and in contrast to the former place of action, this area was ridden with bandit activity well into the end of 1925 and beginning of 1926. Many of those involved in banditry, similarly to in the Polish-Lithuanian region, were former soldiers. Soviet authorities attempted to utilize this unstable political and economic situation, and these bandits, in order to foster discontent amongst the population in Eastern Poland (Nacyjanaĺny Archiŭ Respubliki Bielaruś f. 242p, op. 2, d. 399, 5-6). It was hoped that the newly acquired citizens residing in the borderland regions would become ever more dissatisfied with the ruling Polish regime and be more open to revolutionary change and the propagation of a communist wave through

Poland. Soviet authorities oftentimes hired former German and Polish legionaries for propaganda purposes (Vesialkoŭski 1996, 138). In tangent with Soviet partisan dispatches, leaflets and brochures were disseminated in towns, outlining the evils of the Polish state (Archiwum Akt Nowych Syg. 1278/11, 44).

The official GPU (*Gosudarstvennoe politicheskoe upravlenie*) headquarters in charge of organizing partisan activity were located in Minsk, Moscow, and Kharkiv. The latter comprised three departments: propaganda, operational, and informational. Besides organization at the more official level, Soviet authorities often helped and allowed criminals and unofficial affiliates to easily cross the border into Soviet territory after a raid or incident. Once across the border, it was impossible for Polish authorities to track and apprehend these individuals. In other cases, they recruited or blackmailed individuals to join Soviet partisan groups, especially Polish workers who had crossed the border in search of a job (Zonal'nyi gosudarstvennyi arkhiv Molodechno f. 5, op. 1, d. 60, 3-15). Toward the end of the mid-1920s, however, these same individuals were pillaging villages on both sides of the border.

The Polish government also sent diversionary forces and sometimes even hired individuals on a contractual basis to carry out raids and operations against its eastern neighbour. In the first half of 1921, there were more than 180 such acts perpetrated in the Belarusian Soviet Socialist Republic (BSSR) (Kuźmič 2008, 20). Furthermore, former soldiers of Bulak-Balachovič's army later participated in these Polish-sponsored anti-Soviet campaigns. To combat banditry on its soil, Polish officials dispatched battalions to various hot-spots, increased border security, and relied, albeit unsuccessfully, on intelligence from locals. A special division was created to monitor bandit activity along the border, called the *Korpus Obrony Pograniczny*. The BSSR created its own institution to combat anti-Soviet activity on its soil.

Between May and November of 1921, 360 people were shot by Soviet officials, while 311 were incarcerated as a result of their participation or support of 'insurgent-bandits' (Kuźmič 2008, 21). In the three years following, around one thousand individuals received a similar fate in the BSSR. Another frequent method of trying to prevent banditism was targeting Red Army soldiers with anti-bandit propaganda, encouraging them to stay on fighting, as well as suggesting serious repercussions for their families should they resort to that lifestyle (Nacyjanaĺny Archiŭ Respubliki Bielaruś f. 35, o. 1, f. 183, 34). Following this, those in charge of units in the borderland region were ordered to pursue bandits into swamps. They were also encouraged to break up into smaller groups of 10-15 in order to better track perpetrators (Nacyjanaĺny Archiŭ Respubliki Bielaruś f. 35, o. 1, d. 187, 4-10). By the mid-1920s, the Bolsheviks were setting up anti-bandit headquarters in the areas of Slustk, Breść, and Słonim in order to react and prevent such attacks more efficiently (Nacyjanaĺny Archiŭ Respubliki Bielaruś f. 35, o. 1, f. 188, 22). In Poland, the punishment for membership to such a group was incarceration for no less than eight years, while destruction of the railway or religious and state property could potentially result in a death sentence (Kuźmič 2008, 23).

There were, of course, bandit-related cases and bandit groups beyond the north-eastern provinces of interwar Poland. One of the most organized was the anti-Soviet 'Zialiony Dub' partisan band, instigated after the failed Sluck Uprising, which operated in the BSSR well into the late 1920s. Participants in this group included around five thousand Red Army deserters, as well as members of Bulak-Balachovič's self-proclaimed Belarusian army. Some of those individuals crossing into the BSSR from Poland joined the Zialiony Dub at one point or another (Nacyjanaĺny Archiŭ Respubliki Bielaruś f. 4n, o. 1, d. 16871, 34).[17] Equally, many from the BSSR fled to Poland in order to avoid repercussions by the Soviet state for their participation in anti-Bolshevik armed resistance. While not the focus of this article, keeping in mind the existence of other instances of armed insurgency – and with it, frequent movement of people – depicts a more contextualized landscape of banditism in the borderland region.

## Victims or Avengers? Who Were the Bandits

Hobsbawm addresses the similarities of individuals involved in bandit activity across time and space. While he offers three categories under the larger umbrella of social banditry, the participants' backgrounds are relatively consistent, as are the general environments in which social banditry flourishes. State administrative inefficiency and decentralization cater well to banditry, as this involves remoteness from the central place of power. Those who choose the bandit life usually come from a rural environment, or are men who are not integrated into mainstream society and have been forced out to the margins. This would include, for example, former soldiers and criminals. Some have been victims of injustice or violence and seek vengeful retribution. For others, the bandit-life is more economically and financially safe, seeing as they have no jobs to go back to (Hobsbawm 1985, 60-63).

Narratives of banditry in the north-eastern provinces fit relatively well with Hobsbawm's descriptions. Most of these men were in their early to mid 20s, although there are a few examples of older men joining groups, in their mid to late 40s (Zonal'nyi gosudarstvennyi arkhiv Molodechno f. 5, o. 1, d. 60, 1-15). Many of

---

[17] The most notable figurehead was Ataman Dziarhač (Viačaslaŭ Adamovič), who engaged in anti-Bolshevik activity as late as 1929.

them were former soldiers, mostly from the Polish, Tsarist, or Red Armies, as well as criminals escaping incarceration or sentencing. Some even wore their uniforms while engaging in mischievous activity.

One relatively well-known bandit in the Lida county, Bolesław Żyliński (who used the pseudonym Michał Hajdukiewicz), was a former soldier in the Polish army. During the time when the Bolsheviks occupied Lida in 1920, he hid in the forest with some horses. After their departure, he allegedly tried to return to his unit but was denied because he had lost his paperwork. He returned home to Lida, but after failing to find a job he joined a few other men and began to steal horses, which they would sell in another town. Whenever he was caught by officials or military personnel, he would bribe them with money and was let go. In one case he even gave out 850 tsarist rubles. After doing this, officials would fire twice in the air, giving him the sign to run away (Dziaržaŭny archiŭ Hrodzienskaj voblasci f. 200, v. 1, s. 111, 18-21).

Particular groups garnered more attention due to a well-known nickname for leaders in charge of bands . The label 'Ataman' indicated the leader of a particular group, usually followed by a pseudonym.[18] The number of individuals participating in an act of banditry could be as few as a handful or up to several hundred. Most of them operated on a seasonal schedule, choosing the bandit-partisan life during the warm months of the year and then returning home to their families and home villages in the winter. The most common cases of banditry included home invasions, robberies both in homes and on trains, and murder. Murder was usually a consequence of robbery or looting, although targeted assassinations did exist and were usually carried out against wealthier Poles or Polish government officials. Some instances involved over a hundred partisans essentially taking over an entire town in the middle of the night. With these larger and more coordinated attacks, structured leadership and hierarchy were common. In such a case, the larger group would divide into smaller units, simultaneously targeting the local police, post office, train station, and wealthier inhabitants - usually the 'pans', or Polish aristocrats.

It is the fluidity between personal and bandit life that is noteworthy in the territory in question. There are cases of men engaging in raids and, instead of crossing into Soviet territory for safety, deciding to go home to their wives, or even taking naps in the forest to rest (Nacyjanaĺny Archiŭ Respubliki Bielaruś f. 35, o. 1, f. 188, 32). In reaction to the assassination of a *sejm*, or parliament, representative in February of 1922, along with his wife and three children, *Vilenskoe utro* described the bandits as having been found enjoying some milk on the side of the road and smoking

---

[18] The term ataman first appears in the 13th century, indicating the leader of a Caucus tribe. The term 'ata-man' has been posited to mean father (*otets*) of the people.

Gelma cigarettes (Vilenskoe utro, 19 February 1922, 3). Typically, local reports of banditry did not villainize bandits and instead focused on the embarrassment of local officials or aristocrats. One report in Polesie highlighted the fact that the bandits, while raiding a train car, removed many people's clothing, leaving them only in their undergarments. Alongside many merchants and traders, the mayor was also traveling in the car. In this case there were three casualties, as these individuals had refused to give up their money. It took an hour for the police to arrive after the incident (Nacyjanaĺny Archiŭ Respubliki Bielaruś f. 242n, o. 2, d. 442, 25-27.)

While some reports sought to further highlight the humiliation of government or wealthy officials, other examples in the press demonstrate the frustration and low expectations of locals for their government. In June 1925, after an armed robbery, *Vilenskoe utro* reported that it was the incompetence and corruption of Polish forces that was the problem, as it allowed for the bandits to acquire the weapons used to carry out their attacks (Vilenskoe utro, 5 June 1925, 3). Ordinary locals were also victims of theft, robbery, and even murder at the hands of bandits. On the night of the 26 March 1925, near the river Niemnie in Bielica, a 17-year old boy was murdered in the forest when getting wood for his family. His brother, Antoni, and father, Aleksander, both gave testimonies, but the boy's murderers were never apprehended by the police (Dziaržaŭny archiŭ Hrodzienskaj voblasci f. 200, v. 1, s. 35, 1-15). Such examples evoke Blok's reminder to avoid glorifying bandits; they also highlight the lack of protection locals felt from their governing forces.

Polish authorities were not the only ones derided in this way. The same newspaper poked fun at the Soviet authorities for their plan to infiltrate Polish territory with bandits, as these bandits were now robbing Soviet citizens and causing equal chaos on both sides of the border (Vilenskoe utro, 25 June 1925, 4). After repeated instances of this, Soviet authorities began organizing and dispatching anti-bandit units to the border and tried to dissuade locals from helping them (Nacyjanaĺny Archiŭ Respubliki Bielaruś Belarus' f. 35, o. 1, d. 183, 34). A trend emerged in which papers reported a bandit incident and then issued statements stressing that, as per usual, army and police forces had failed to alleviate the situation (Krynica, 1 March 1925, 3).

These examples illustrate both Hobsbawm and Blok's ideas, namely, that the focus on bandits as an expression of peasant sentiment is an interesting one, but it is a relationship that should not be elevated or glorified. People's distrust of the state was twofold – due to both the repression against them and the ruling government's inability to protect them from crime. Thus, bandits become not strictly good or bad. They are also not political, but merely an anti-government entity and at times a manifestation of the people's frustrations.

## Ataman Mucha as an Allegorical Figure

While both petty and serious crimes were seemingly ubiquitous in these regions in the early 1920s, one image became especially pervasive – that of Ataman Mucha. Although stories of his alleged acts of terror and charity were repeated and immortalized, there is little hard evidence concerning the individual himself. Valiancin Panamaroŭ has claimed that Mucha was a pseudonym for a Soviet partisan by the name of Arloŭski[19] (Panamaroŭ 1983, 22). In the archival collection of the Communist Party of West Belarus in Minsk, Arloŭski and Mucha are two separate individuals, labelled as Soviet partisans of the 1920s (Nacyjanaĺny Archiŭ Respubliki Bielaruś f. 242p, o. 1, d. 599, 237-239). Other scholars have posited that Mucha was the name of an anti-Polish bandit group, and not a specific individual. One historian describes Mucha as merely a cryptic name utilized by multiple partisan leaders in West Belarus, borrowed from an officer who deserted the Polish Army (Kandybovič 2000, 147).

The most detailed biographical account of the alleged Mucha comes from one Soviet partisan, Stanislav Alekseevich Vaupshasov,[20] who claims that Mucha was in fact a real individual. According to Vaupshasov's autobiographical account, Mucha-Michalski's real name was Šabloŭski, and he had deserted his officer post in the Polish Army. He was found by Arloŭski hiding in the forest and was taken in as a member of their Soviet partisan group. Vaupshasov notes that Mucha was a huge asset to the band. He was disciplined due to his military training, and furthermore, he spoke Polish well, which allowed them to carry out operations more efficiently. Most of the time, he merely used his language skill to instruct locals or train passengers on what exactly to do – essentially, stay calm and hand over their valuables (Vaupshasov 1965, 16). Furthermore, Arloŭski hoped a Polish officer joining a Soviet partisan band would worry the Polish government, as stories of Mucha and his background would further validate local opinions of the government. In order to catalyse this fear, Arloŭski and other members of the group, including Vaupshasov himself, decided to use Mucha's name when perpetrating acts collectively or even separately.

The Poles became concerned about Mucha in 1922, and in May of that year, an investigation began into his background. The local state police in Będzina was

---

[19]　Kiryl Prakofjevič Arloŭski (1895 – 1968) was born in Myškavičy (Mahilioŭ region, BSSR). He served as a non-commissioned officer during the First World War, and then ordered to create a partisan an anti-German partisan unit. His efforts then shifted to an anti-Polish partisan unit. He later worked for the People's Commissariat of Internal Affairs (NKVD) from 1925 to 1937 and was later involved in anti-Franco missions during the Spanish Civil War. During the Great Patriotic War, he led the Falcon partisan unit, active in the Baranovichi oblast. He was subsequently awarded many honors for is service.

[20]　Stanislav Alekseevich Vaupshasov (1899-1976) was born in Gruzdžiai, present-day Lithuania. In 1918 he volunteered for the Red Army and in the 1920s was active in the anti-Polish, Soviet partisan movement. He was later active in the Civil War in Spain, within the anti-Franco armed resistance. During the Great Patriotic War, he worked in the cheka and established relations with the partisan movement and was later active in it. He was subsequently awarded with many honors for his service.

ordered to investigate his family in Jawożnik. By this time, they were aware that he went by another name – Michaĺski - and wanted to know if there had been any correspondence between him and his parents. In the meantime, police units were to arrest him on accounts of being a 'dangerous bandit', having killed a few people, and for having deserted the Polish army. He was reported to be 24 years old (as of 24 May 1922) and had joined the Polish army on 12 November 1918 as part of the 6th Mounted Rifles Regiment, stationed in Lwów. He was described as a man of medium height with a round face, dark-blond hair, and blue eyes. The report stressed that, if found and caught, Mucha was to be escorted by heavily armed guards into the nearest police station (Dziaržaŭny archiŭ Hrodzienskaj voblasci f. 679, v. 1, s. 3, 46-47).

While the biographical lacuna in Mucha's life leaves us with a murky narrative, it is the myths, stories, and legends regarding him that have proved to be powerful and significant. The largely peasant environment, governed distantly by the state, created an atmosphere that was conducive to banditism. However, the oral stories, myths, and legends surrounding Mucha transcended the local population and his mysterious whereabouts synthesized a figure that everyone could relate to and admire. Hobsbawm makes this argument and stresses that the appeal that bandits have has always gone beyond their native environment (Hobsbawm 1985, 131). In the case of Mucha, the appeal was one that did not only transcend geographical spaces within the borderlands, but also people's national and ethnic backgrounds. Papers of various political and socio-economic perspectives mentioned Mucha in an awestruck, if not positive light.

The stories surrounding Mucha lauded him for the near-impossible tasks that he was able to pull off, while successfully escaping repercussions. *Vilenskoe slovo* stated that

> ... even the police cannot catch him, because in Galicja they are not taught how to catch this Eskimo from the Lithuanian forests. Perhaps it is because they only use sticky paper, which usually works for a variety of flies that fly around in a room. But this particular fly is not like that. In the meantime, Mucha is healthy and merry all throughout the *kresy* and continues to gain popularity in his Belovezha nest. (Nacyjanaĺny Archiŭ Respubliki Bielaruś f. 242p, o. 2, d. 442, 33).

The most frequently reported good deed by Mucha was redistribution of monetary funds to locals from the pockets of local officials and wealthy residents. *Vilenskoe utro* reported that Mucha sent letters to local government officials in Oszmiana, as well as to the head of police and a local millionaire, demanding a sum of 35 million Polish marks to be delivered for redistribution to local people (Nacyjanaĺny Archiŭ Respubliki Bielaruś f. 242p, o. 2, d. 442, 39-40). The purpose was to alleviate the locals of the heavy taxes they had to pay to the Polish government. In another operation, on 19 January 1923 in Czuczewicze, Mucha and his 40-man crew successfully stole 40 million marks from the bank, along with police officers' uniforms, and escaped unscathed. The police were then embarrassingly forced to seek help from the neighbouring town, walking in their undergarments.

In another anecdote, Mucha's actions are less heroic. After having successfully raided a town, Mucha and his men wanted to scare the local priest. They placed a backpack on him and told him to stay still, because it was filled with grenades. The priest remained in an uncomfortable position for hours before he was found, only to discover that the backpack had been filled with potatoes (Śleszyński 2005, 26). The report, however, does not mention Mucha's crew, but rather focuses on the poor priest, whose 'faithful' followers had forgotten him for several hours, forcing him to stand so long.

Besides accounts of robberies and humiliation of local officials, narratives of his charming personality were equally popular. *Rzeczpospolita* reported that

> this *kresovy* Rinaldo-Rinaldini[21] usually travels with a group of 10 to 12 men and skirts around the border area. All his ambushes are similar in nature. He catches a party of people just about to sit down for dinner, but before they can eat, Mucha enters the dining room. He asks the individuals to sit and to remain calm and unafraid, for he does not intend to cause anyone any harm. Since many of these people are usually women, the well-mannered Mucha introduces himself with a graceful smile. Once he takes the adequate amount of money and valuables, he then asks for a friendly cup of tea, after which he kisses his hosts' hands and thanks them with a bow. Soon after, the well-behaved young man disappears, eluding the police. Two weeks later he appears where they least expect him (Stepek and Hoffman-Krystyańczyk 1923, 194).

Polish authorities were not blind to Mucha's popularity. In an instructional rulebook for police forces, the authors included a section on how to deal with bandits. Mucha's name comes up with a description of his immense popularity with the locals, and especially young boys, who admire him and inform him of everything that goes on (Stepek and Hoffman-Krystyańczyk 1923, 195). No official resolution as to how to deal with bandits is provided. Furthermore, Mucha's reach went beyond the youth. *Słowo* reported:

---

[21] Rinaldo Rinaldini is a literary figure in a 1797 novel by Christian August Vulpius entitled, *Rinaldo Rinaldini, der Räuberhauptmann.* He was known as the 'bandit of bandits'. The popular novel inspired theatrical performances and even the production of a German silent-film in 1927, directed by Max Obal and Rudolf Dworsky. There was even a Franco-German television series inspired by Rinaldini in 1968, entitled *La kermesse des brigands.*

The fact that a major thief, who grew up among Belarusian peasants, does not have any peasant qualities, makes him more likeable to the inhabitants of Aŭguscinaŭ, Nadniomansk, Belastok, Ružansk, Bielavieža, Naliboki, and Paliessk. He plays with our authorities, jokes with the police, behaves like a gentleman, and from time to time he lunches at the Varšavianka in Vilnius. All of this increases his influence amongst Belarusian peasants (Nacyjanaĺny Archiŭ Respubliki Bielaruś f. 242p, o. 2, d. 442, 33).

*Kurier Polski* wrote an article entitled 'Ataman Mucha – a warning'. The article discusses, in detail, the chaos committed by Mucha, but it then reports that, even with his busy schedule, he managed to pay taxes in Navahrudak. By the end of the piece, the author admits that Mucha is likeable to Polish peasants, because they relate to him more than they do to their own police, whom they perceive as foreigners (Nacyjanaĺny Archiŭ Respubliki Bielaruś f. 242p, o. 2, d. 442, 35-36).

Looking at these excerpts and snippets from local papers offers entertaining anecdotes and perceptions of bandits by locals. Beyond providing us with an idea of these sentiments in the north-eastern Polish territory during the 1920s, this narrative offers us a window into the post-war lives of everyday people. Through these stories and opinions, we see a population trying to overcome economic struggles, while also being indifferent or hostile to post-war political restructuring. The state, whether Lithuania, Poland, or Soviet Russia, seem to be seen as a collective entity and more importantly, continuously taking advantage of local inhabitants. In this world of chaos and uncertainty, tales of those disrupting state-building efforts were welcomed. Nevertheless, Mucha's story highlights the fact that the likeability of these bandit-partisans were not uni-dimensional, or merely anti-state in nature. Mucha's sophistication and charm are admired just as much as his sabotage of railways and humiliation of local government officials. Through the representation of Mucha, we see a local distaste for government institutions, but also desire for entertainment and comic relief. Historiographically, this perspective also dismantles categories and labels such as 'anti-Polish' or 'Soviet', or 'anti-Soviet', as we see these lines as murky and unclear. In many ways, Mucha – the man, the myth, and the memory – serves as an allegory of locality and identity at this time, which is not fixed within any ethnic or national mould.

Mucha's identity combined an element of relatability, as well as admiration, and became an image that would retain its appeal beyond the 1920s. Hobsbawm notes that:

> ...The bandits belonged to remembered history, as distinct from the official history of books. They are part of the history which is not so much a record of events and those who shaped them, as of the

symbols of the theoretically controllable but actually uncontrolled factors which determine the world of the poor: of just kings and men who bring justice to the people. That is why the bandit legend still has power to move us. (Hobsbawm 1985, 133).

It is this glimpse into the 'world of the poor' that can offer us a better understanding of history from below, which in the multi-ethnic and fluid region of West Belarus, cannot be explained strictly through archival documents and facts. It is a world that goes beyond neat categorization or classification and thus necessitates the use of an alternative frame through which to untangle the intricate elements of its history.

## The Decline of Banditism

After the diplomatic settlement of the borders of Eastern Poland, security on the frontier tightened. It became increasingly hard to escape repercussions, both in Poland and in Soviet Russia. The fate of these bandits went in several directions. Many of them were captured and faced repercussions. Those engaged in anti-Soviet campaigns, including those after the failed Sluck uprising, were either caught in the 1920s, or in some cases, managed to live in the BSSR unnoticed. One such group, led by former Bulak-Balachovič soldiers Iosif Zinievič and Ihar Piańkoŭski, worked on anti-Soviet operations and managed to remain in the BSSR until 1937 and 1938, when their group was dissolved (Nacyjanaĺny Archiŭ Respubliki Bielaruś f. 4п, o. 1, d. 1687, 32-36). Those that had allegedly been anti-Polish partisans sought refuge and lived for a time in the BSSR. Their lives would later be jeopardized in the 1930s, during the purges and repression that sent many to labour camps or to be executed. The argument was that, even though they had fought in service of the Soviet state, they had been exposed to bourgeois, Polish capitalist ways, and hence posed a danger to the regime. A few luckier individuals became partisans in the following Second World War, Arloŭski and Vaupshasov being two of them, both receiving the Hero of the Soviet Union honour.

As for Mucha, his story seems to end just as mysteriously as his life was. In Maladečna, there is a record of a Michal Sukhov claiming to be Mucha. Sukhov and his friend were both arrested and given a death sentence; however, only the friend's death certificate exists (Zonal'nyi gosudarstvennyi arkhiv Molodechno f. 111, o. 2, d. 195, 10). Using Mucha's name was not unusual and in fact, some Belarusian nationalist fighters would later use it for their personal pseudonyms during the Second World War.

Jerzy Paciorkowski offers another anecdote from Mucha's fate. After a train ambush and robbery on 4 November 1923, a combined police effort from the areas of BaranaviČy, Niasviž, and Luniniec managed to track part of Mucha's crew. As can be predicted, the Lithuanian Eskimo was not one of those apprehended. He presumably fled to Soviet Russia after which there is no recorded evidence of his existence nor any concrete, verified sighting.


## Concluding Thoughts

Since the publication of Hobsbawm's work on social banditry, his analytical model has been used and deconstructed, adapting to particular cases in global contexts. As scholars focus on different regions of their particular cases to either confirm or reject tenets of Hobsbawm's work, what is clear is that it still serves as a foundational basis from which more questions can be formulated. While his work and framework can be utilized universally, each case is universally chiral. Each region experiences a particular history that shapes society, including peasants, allowing for different types of 'bandits' to exist. Concepts of Hobsbawm and Blok's theories offer a starting point; however, they are not meant to be complete explanations or categorizations for every case that exists.

In its discussion of banditry and the narrative of Ataman Mucha in the north-eastern interwar Polish regions, this article does not completely embrace, nor refute Hobsbawm's model. It utilizes bandits to explore a region that in the 1920s was largely apolitical, one that experienced multiple cruel occupational regimes, and then struggled in a period of post-war economic chaos and instability. Bandit life offered a means of survival for some, despite efforts by the Polish and Soviet state to politicize and utilize these groups for their goals. While some armed groups may have been more ideologically inclined, they were not perceived this way by locals. Furthermore, despite atrocities committed by bandits, the state was blamed for its inability to defend its citizens.

Looking at the history of the region, in addition to post-war banditry and its perception, what is apparent is that the region continued to be destabilized, even after the war. Furthermore, 'war' continued to exist, as did the struggle for survival. The bandit and his representation in local papers was not a characteristic of pre-political protest, nor of a uniform peasant resistance, but a manifestation of anti-government sentiments, resulting from the frustrations of locals who, perhaps, sought a life in an enclave, distant from occupational centres of power.

FIGURE 1: Józef Mucha-Michalski (? - ?)
Photograph of the alleged Mucha, identified as a soviet partisan, in the National Archives
of the Republic of Belarus (NARB f. 242p, v. 1, s. 599, p. 237)

FIGURE 2: Kiryl Prakofjevič Arloŭski, 1895-1968
(NARB f. 242p, v. 1, s. 599, p. 239)

FIGURE 3:Stanislav Vaupshasov, 1899-1976
(NARB f. 242p, v. 1, s. 599, p. 227)

FIGURE 4: Niasviž, Belarus
Memorial to Polish police officers, who fell victim to a bandit ambush on 30 March 1926
(From personal collection)

## References

Archiwum Akt Nowych (AAN) Syg. 1278/11: *Armia Czerwona – zbiór akt, 1917-1922.*

Bartov, O. and Weitz E., 2013. *Shatterzones of Empires: Coexistence and Violence in the German, Habsburg, Russian, and Ottoman Borderlands.* Bloomington: Indiana University Press.

Blok, Anton, 1972. "The Peasant and the Brigand: Social Banditry Reconsidered." *Comparative Studies in Society and History,* vol. 14, no. 4, pp. 494-503.

Böhler, J., Borodziej, W., von Puttkamer, J, eds., 2014. *Legacies of Violence: Eastern Europe's First World War.* München, Oldenbourg Verlag.

Brown, K., 2003. *A Biography of No Place: From Ethnic Borderland to Soviet Heartland.* Cambridge: Harvard University Press.

Cichoracki, Piotr, 2012. *Stołpce-Łowcza-Leśna 1924: II Rzeczypospolita wobec najpoważniejszych incydentów zbrojnych w województwach północno-wschodnich.* Łomianki: Wydawnictwo LTW.

Dziarzhaŭny arkhiŭ Hrodzienskai voblasti f. 200, v. 1, s. 35.

Dziarzhaŭny arkhiŭ Hrodzienskai voblasti f. 200, v. 1, s. 111.

Dziarzhaŭny arkhiŭ Hrodzienskai voblasti f. 679, v. 1, s. 3

Hobsbawm, E.J., 1981. *Bandits.* New York: Pantheon Books.

Isaacman, Allen, 1977. "Social Banditry in Zimbabwe (Rhodesia) and Mozambique 1894-1907: an Expression of Early Peasant Protest", *Journal of Southern African Studies 4,* no. 1. Special issue on Protest and Resistance, pp. 1-30.

Jorš, S., 1998. Lehiendarny Ataman (Artykul pra Jakuba Chareŭskaha), *Naša Niva,* 15 (112).

Kandybovič, S., 2000. *Razhrom Nacyjanalnaha Ruchu ŭ Bielarusi.* Minsk: Bielaruski Histaryčny Ahliad.

Kowalski, Zdzisław G. 1998. "Granica Ryska", in Mieczysław Wojciechowski ed., *Traktat ryski 1921 roku po 75 latach,* Toruń: Wydawnictwo Uniwersytetu Mikołaja Kopernika, pp. 127-139.

Krynica, 1925. *U Polśčy,* nr. 9, 1 March.

Kuźmič, V., 2008. Baraćba z nieliehalnymi ŭzbrojenymi farmiravanniami na bielaruskim uchastku saviecka-polskaha pamiežža (1921-1926 hh), *Bielaruski Histaryčny Časopis,* 18–26.

Mironowicz, Eugeniusz, 2007. *Białorusini i Ukraińcy w polityce obozu piłsudczykowskiego.* Białystok: Wydawnictwo Uniwersyteckie.

Mironowicz, Eugeniusz, 1999. *Białoruś – Historia Państw Świata w XX Wieku.* Warszawa: Wydawnictwo Trio.

Nacyjanaĺny Archiŭ Respubliki Bielaruś f. 4п, v. 1, s. 16871.

Nacyjanaĺny Archiŭ Respubliki Bielaruś f. 35, v. 1, s. 183.

Nacyjanaĺny Archiŭ Respubliki Bielaruś f. 35, v. 1, s. 187.

Nacyjanaĺny Archiŭ Respubliki Bielaruś f. 35, v. 1, s. 188.

Nacyjanaĺny Archiŭ Respubliki Bielaruś f. 242p, v. 1, s. 599.

Nacyjanaĺny Archiŭ Respubliki Bielaruś f. 242p, v. 2, s. 442.

Nacyjanaĺny Archiŭ Respubliki Bielaruś f. 242p, v. 2, s. 399.

Paciorkowski, J., 2014. *Watażka z Kresów.* Available at: <http://www.gazeta.policja.pl/997/archiwum-1/2014/numer-110-052014/98399,Watazka-z-Kresow.print.> [Accessed 8 March 2016].

Panamaroŭ, V., 1983. *Kiryla Arloŭski: Dakumientaĺnaja apaviesć.* Minsk: Junactva.

Poluian, V. and Poluian I., 1962. *Revolutsionnoe i natsionalno-ocvoboditelnoe dvizhenie v zapadnoi Belorussii.* Minsk: Gosudarstvennoe izdatelstvo BSSR.

Prusin, A., 2010. *The Lands Between: Conflict in the East European Borderlands, 1870-1992.* New York: Oxford University Press.

Rudling, Per Anders, 2015. *The Rise and Fall of Belarusian Nationalism, 1906-1931.* Pittsburgh: University of Pittsburgh Press.

Scott, J., 2009. *The Art of Not Being Governed: An Anarchist History of Upland Southeast Asia.* New Haven, Yale University Press.

Singelmann, Peter, 1975. "Political Structure and Social Banditry in Northeast Brazil." *Journal of Latin American Studies,* vol. 7, no 1, pp. 59-83.

Slatta, Richard W., 2004. "Eric J. Hobsbawm's Social Bandit: A Critique and Revision," *A Contracorriente: A Journal on Social History and Literature in Latin America* 1, no. 2, pp. 1-30.

Sorokin, A., 1970. *Osvoboditelnoe i revolutsionnoe krestianskoe dvizhenie v Zapadnoi Belorussii 1920-1939.* Minsk: Izdatelstvo BGU im. V.I. Lenina.

Stasievič, J., 1995. Partyzanka Zachodniaj Bielarusi, *Pahonia*, no. 12(111), pp. 1–8.

Stepek, W. and Hoffmann-Krystyańczyk, Z., 1923. *Służba Śledcza: podręcznik dla organów bezpieczeństwa za 49 rycinami.* Poznań: Nakładem Księgarni Fr. Gutowskiego.

Stużyńska, N., 1999. "Antysowiecka konspiracja i partyzantka Zielonego Dębu na terenie Białorusi w latach 1919-1925," in R. Jasiewicz, ed., *Europa Nieprowincjonalna.* Warsaw and London: Instytut Studiów Politycznych PAN, pp. 859-866.

Stuzhynskaia, N., 2009. "Ataman Grach: v teni 'Zielonoho duba'", *Dedy: daidzhest publikatsii o belaruskoi istorii/sostavlenie i nauchnoie redaktirovanie A.E. Tarasa.* Minsk: A.N. Varaksin.

Stużynskaja, Nina., 2012. *Bielaruś Miacieżnaja: z historyi ŭzbrojenaha antysavieckaha supracivu ŭ1920-ja hh.* Minsk: Vydavec A.M. Varaksin.

Śleszyński, W., 2005. *Walka instytucji państwowych z białoruską działalnością dywersyjną 1920-1925.* Białystok: Polskie Towarzystwo Historyczne.

Vaupshasov, S., 1965. *Na razgnevannoi zemle.* Minsk: Izdatel'stvo "Belarus'".

Vesialkoŭski, Jury, 1996. *Bielarus' u Pieršaj Susvietnaj vajnie.* Belastok i London.

Vilenskoe utro, 1922. *Ubiistvo semi chelovek,* no. 130, 19 February.

Vilenskoe utro, 1925. *Na granitse,* no. 1339, 25 June.

Wróbel, Piotr, 2010. "The Rise and Fall of Parliamentary Democracy in Interwar Poland," in M.B.B. Biskupski, James S. Pula, and Piotr J. Wróbel eds., *The Origins of Modern Polish Democracy,* Athens: Oxford University Press, 110-164.

Zonal'nyi gosudarstvennyi arkhiv v. g. Molodechno f. 111, op. 2, d. 195.

Zonal'nyi gosudarstvennyi arkhiv v. g. Molodechno f. 5, op. 1, d. 60.

Żarnowski, Janusz, 1973. *Społeczeństwo Drugiej Rzeczypospolitej 1918-1939.* Warszawa: Państwowe Wydawnictwo Naukowe.

# When Autocracies Have
# No Respect for the Nobel Prize

BY

INA SHAKHRAI

As both the first writer and the first woman from Belarus to receive the Nobel Prize in Literature, Svetlana Alexievich became a centre of public attention worldwide. While the first tweets from the Nobel announcement room generated some confusion regarding this unknown writer from an unknown land – with about '10,000 reporters googling Svetlana Alexievich' (Brooks 2015) – the subsequent media coverage of the writer in such publications as *The Guardian*, *The New Yorker*, and *Der Spiegel* sketched out a broad picture of Alexievich's life, career and main works.

Meanwhile, the Belarusian state media remained reluctant to give the award much attention: the upcoming presidential elections and Lukashenka's visit to Turkmenistan took priority. In a couple of cafes and art spaces in Minsk young people gathered to watch Alexievich's speech live via the Internet. Independent and alternative websites offered platforms for discussion and the exchange of opinions. Interestingly, the general public was divided over the question of the 'Belarusianness' of Alexievich. The identity of the protagonist in Alexievich's books caused a heated discussion among Russian intellectuals as well. They could hardly accept that Alexievich's works might epitomize the experience of a genuinely Soviet individual, as they set out to. There was also much speculation on whether Alexievich should be acknowledged as a Russian writer, or whether the West treated her as Belarusian in order to chastise Russia.

The events surrounding Alexievich's Nobel Prize represent a revealing example of the all-encompassing nature of autocratic political systems, as well as how confusing and interwoven national identities can be. Researcher Volha Charnysh explains the controversial reactions to Alexievich's Nobel Prize in Belarus by pointing out the growing politicisation of language choice and interpretation of history. According to her, in the Belarusian cultural sphere 'both the regime's opponents and supporters alike practice the denunciation of writers who do not follow the political script' and remain 'prisoners to Belarus's Soviet past and authoritarian present' (Charnysh 2015a). Moreover, contrasting reactions to Alexievich's work 'reflect deepening divisions in post-Soviet space' and indicate the weakness of national identity in Belarus (Charnysh 2015b). Lizaveta Kasmach underlines the relevance of the role of Belarusian society, which, unlike the pro-governmental mass media and the authorities, treated Alexievich 'with the appropriate recognition and respect' (2016).

This article stresses the interconnection between the current political situation in Belarus, Soviet history and the post-Soviet region. Using the case of Alexievich's Nobel Prize, it analyses how autocratic elites learn from the past, and how diffused norms shape public attitudes in neighbouring autocracies. The article assumes that the choice of the Belarusian authorities to strategically neglect Alexievich's contribution to the Belarusian cultural landscape, as well as the prevalence of nationalist discourse surrounding Alexievich's Nobel prize in both Belarus and Russia, are conditioned by the geographical proximity of Belarus and Russia and their common historical past. Therewith it contributes to research on autocracy, elaborates on the learning of autocratic practices across space and time, and expands on the knowledge of contemporary politics in Belarus and Russia. This research is based on both primary sources, such as official statements, opinion poll data, and media coverage, and secondary sources, such as analytical articles and papers.

The unusual post-modern format of Alexievich's works naturally raised many questions among scholars, writers and readers. However, this study will not discuss the literary quality and value of Alexievich's writing, leaving this task for literary critics.

The article is organised as follows: It first introduces the concept of autocratic learning. It then analyses how the perception of Alexievich's Nobel Prize by the Belarusian authorities mirrored the treatment of disloyal intellectuals in the Soviet tradition. It also elaborates on the attitudes of Belarusian civil society towards Alexievich's award. The paper then goes on to examine the diffusion of nationalist sentiment in Belarusian and Russian society, and the resulting controversial attitudes towards Alexievich as a Nobel Winner. Finally, it concludes that Alexievich has not become a unifying figure for the post-Soviet community.

## Autocratic Learning

The dynamics of external-internal diffusion processes and their impact on national political regimes 'have received scant attention in the literature' (Lankina and others 2016). Therefore, scholars of the new autocracy studies increasingly focus on the external dimension of authoritarianism and on the diffusion of authoritarian norms and practices across space and time. Along with the active promotion of autocracy, such issues as 'regime-boosting regionalism' (Melnykovska and others 2012; Erdmann and others 2013), mutual learning among autocracies (Silitski 2010; Vanderhill 2012) or unintended autocratic impact (Obydenkova and Libman

2015), have appeared on the research agenda. This study contributes to literature on unintentional authoritarian impact through autocratic learning.

Autocratic learning, alternatively called lesson-drawing, is a mechanism of norms diffusion, through which external actors unintentionally influence domestic political processes. Heydemann and Leenders define it as a 'wave effect facilitated by the rapid diffusion of ideas, discourses, and practices from one country to another and their adaptation to local contexts' (2011, p. 648). The researchers initially applied this concept to study the protests in the Arab world in the 2010s both on the level of Arab societies and on the level of autocratic elites, focusing especially on the elites' response to social unrest. In his paper for the workshop 'International Diffusion and Cooperation of Authoritarian Regimes' held in Hamburg, Germany, in 2016, Leenders fine-tuned his definition to include the notion of autocratic resilience. According to his new definition, autocratic learning should be understood as a set of 'international and transnational interactions enabling the exchange or transfer of knowledge, ideas, insights, models, expertise, skills and/or technology that can be used at the service of a regime's efforts to adjust, enhance or optimize authoritarian governance' (Leenders 2016).

The analysis of autocratic learning and the unintended consequences of external influence ignores the intentions and goals of a political actor, whose mere existence can cause changes in the policies of a potential recipient. Therefore, it focuses primarily on the ability of domestic actors to watch and learn from their own historical experience and from the experience of their neighbours, and to adapt the lessons learned to local circumstances. Even if this theoretical constraint seriously limits the scope of the article, for the purpose of this research it is important to concentrate on unintentional, often unforeseen consequences, rather than on the coordinated efforts of politicians.

The process of learning, or lesson-drawing, occurs through the following processes: adoption, which is conceptualised as a direct and complete copying of foreign norms, ideas, practices or models; emulation, or an adoption with adjustments to domestic circumstances; and inspiration - a process that occurs when external norms, ideas, practices or models inspire change, but with a final outcome not drawn from foreign examples (McFaul and others 2009, 17). These lessons can be drawn from various actors, including neighbouring states, predecessor states, or leading international actors. The effectiveness of learning as an unintentional diffusion process is higher for those actors who find themselves 'in geographic proximity or who share cultural or economic links' (Ambrosio 2013, 197-98). The assessment of a learning outcome is made on the basis of the references to the lessons learned, as well as adoption and adaptation facts and convergence[1] of policies.

---

[1] Convergence here involves different degrees of movement towards conformity with the pre-existing point of reference (a powerful state, a regional organization or even a community) (McFaul and others 2009, 10).

Belarus represents a revealing case study of autocratic learning due to its geographical proximity to Russia, its Soviet past and current political regime. Recent examples of how autocratic elites in Belarus have learned from neighbouring actors include, among others, the use of the apple blossom ribbon instead of the Russian St. Georgian ribbon on Victory Day, or the copying of certain legal provisions from repressive Russian laws on mass media activity in the context of the Ukrainian crisis since autumn 2013. This article uses the specific case of the reception of Alexievich's Nobel Prize in Belarus and Russia to demonstrate both the learning effect among political elites and the diffusion of autocratic norms across communities and civil society.

## The Perception of Alexievich's Nobel Prize in Belarus

### *The Reluctance of Autocratic Elites in Belarus with Regard to the Nobel Prize*

The fact that Lukashenka, his retainers, and the official media in Belarus initially attempted to ignore or downplay the celebration of Alexievich's prize can be explained by the writer's critical stance towards current Belarusian and Russian regimes and towards their common Soviet heritage. Belarusian officials learned from the Soviet leadership's discriminatory treatment of disloyal intellectuals. In the case of Alexievich, they have taken recourse in the strategy of neglect and even tacit condemnation of the significance of Alexievich's works. Indeed, the degree of self-censorship which was reflected in the eagerness of bureaucrats and officials to pointedly ignore or deride Alexievich resembled the Soviet tradition of treating 'untrustworthy' intellectuals and public figures in this way.

Why would Alexievich be perceived as disloyal or even garner comparisons with Bunin or Pasternak? First of all, her difficult relationship with Belarusian and Russian authorities has a long history. As both a literary writer and an investigative journalist, she covered many sensitive issues such as the Chernobyl catastrophe, the Soviet war in Afghanistan, and female soldiers in WWII. Subsequent close attention from both Soviet and Belarusian authorities in regard to her personality was thus inevitable.

Consequently, Alexievich did not receive any recognition in Belarus or win any Belarusian literary prizes, despite being a winner of numerous international awards, including ones from Russia and the USSR. In one of her first interviews after receiving the Nobel Prize, she complained: 'The Belarusian authorities pretend that I don't exist. My books are not published, I can't speak anywhere, at least on Belarusian television' (Alexievich 2015a). Indeed, she has not been published in Belarus for almost 25 years, while 500 copies of her recent book *Second-hand Time* were published by a quasi-underground non-state publisher called Lohvinau (Hulpachova 2015).

Partly in protest against the authoritarian politics of Lukashenka, partly 'to save her energies for writing' (Gessen 2015), Alexievich left Belarus in 2000 and lived in France, Germany, Italy, and Sweden for more than ten years. Professedly, she hoped to wait for the autocratic regime in Belarus to democratise, but unwilling to wait that long she returned to Minsk. As she put it herself: 'I was wrong to think I could sit him out' (Gessen 2015).

Alexievich has made open and direct statements about her attitude to authoritarian regimes. In her last book, *Second-hand Time*, she created a collective image of a Soviet person with the voices of the witnesses to Soviet time. She comes to the conclusion that, as she stated later in her interviews, 'the heaviest heritage of socialism is a man, a traumatised man because a camp perverts both the hangman and the victim' (Alexievich 2015a). Interestingly, in the book she 'identifies explicitly (by using "we") with her own generation, 'simultaneously Soviet and post-Soviet" (Snyder 2015). In this vein, her criticism of the current regimes in Belarus and Russia is interconnected with the traumatic experience of the Soviet past.

Alexievich has called Belarus a 'soft dictatorship' (*Deutsche Welle* 2015) and criticised Lukashenka for the absence of a political will to carry out reforms, and for his obsession with power (*Govorit Moskva* 2015). She has also condemned authoritarian policies in Russia (Alexievich 2015a), as well as recent political developments in the country, including, among others, the intervention in Ukraine and the annexation of Crimea (Charter97.org 2015). Despite the fact that the Russian Minister of Information was one of the first to congratulate Alexievich on her Nobel Prize, the Russian authorities have mostly ignored developments surrounding her accomplishment. The reactions of the authorities in Belarus have reflected disappointment regarding their unfulfilled expectations that as a Nobel Prize Winner, Alexievich would take advantage of her international podium to show loyalty and support for the official regime.

On 8 October 2015, several hours after the announcement of the Nobel Prize Winner in Literature, Lukashenka congratulated Alexievich (The official internet portal of the President of the Republic of Belarus 2015b). Later, during a press-conference in Berlin on 11 October 2015, Alexievich noted: 'President Gauck was the first person to congratulate me, then the foreign minister, and in the evening Lukashenka congratulated me. That was a bit strange' (*Ukraine Today* 2015). However, this was not the only time that Lukashenka recognised the achievements of Alexievich in public. Later, when being asked about his attitude to Alexievich during a meeting with the construction workers of the Belarusian nuclear power plant, Lukashenka answered:

> I'm glad for her, as she is a citizen of Belarus. The award means that, regardless of your position, you can still work and create, write,

speak your mind and so on in Belarus. [...] I've read her thoughts in the printed media, which I daily receive. [...] In my greeting to Ms. Alexievich, I wrote that it's important that a Belarusian has won a Nobel Prize: the first time since Soviet days. The key now is how she'll use this. [...] You may be flying high, but how will you use this image, this legacy? For the benefit of your people? People should enjoy the benefit of you being fortunate enough to receive this award; we'll survive any sort of oppositional thoughts (2015b).

During an informal talk with the Swedish ambassador Oberg, Lukashenka again stressed that Alexievich didn't represent any political opposition, and ordered her books to be presented to the ambassador on his behalf (Kalesnikava 2015). The cautious benevolence of Lukashenka was clearly based on the expectation that Alexievich would use her sudden international visibility to attract positive attention to Belarus and improve its image. However, very soon Lukashenka faced Alexievich's criticism and disparagement, and the official tactics for dealing with the Nobel Prize winner changed.

The day after the conversation with the Swedish ambassador, during an event dedicated to the Russian composer Drobysh, Lukashenka spoke unfavourably about Alexievich. He accused her of pouring 'a bucket of mud on the country' and called her a 'bad son' of her homeland (Belsat 2015a). Since then, Belarusian officials and the state media have mostly neglected the events following her Nobel Prize win. Thus, Belarusian TV refused to broadcast the Nobel Lecture on 7 December, as well as the Nobel Prize Award Ceremony and Banquet Speech on 10 December, citing technical and financial difficulties (*Belaruspartisan* 2015).

The pro-government newspaper *Belarus Segodnia* attempted to portray Alexievich's loyal stance toward the current Belarusian authorities and published some excerpts from Alexievich's Nobel lecture, acknowledging that the scale of her achievement would in the end benefit the global image of Belarus. An unsigned editorial commentary concluded that she 'was not willing to follow the lead of so-called "pseudo-democrats,"' which they inferred from the lack of references to any opposition slogans in her lecture (*Belarus Segodnya* 2015). However, already on the day after the publication of this article, Alexievich in her Banquet speech spoke in Belarusian about the autocratic policies in the country (Alexievich 2015c).

### Belarusian Civil Society Celebrates the Nobel Prize

While Belarusian officials and the state media remained passive and unenthusiastic about the first Belarusian Nobel Prize winner, Belarusians themselves demonstrated an impressive level of civic self-organisation. Thus, 'as a response to the state's disdain of Belarus's Nobel Laureate,' the Facebook initiative 'Let's celebrate the Nobel together!' and the hashtag #nobelrazam were born (Kuchta 2015). In a number of cafes and art spaces in Minsk, young people gathered to watch the ceremony and Alexievich's speech live via the Internet. Independent and alternative websites offered platforms for discussion and the exchange of opinions. Around 300 people came to the National Airport to greet Alexievich when she returned from Sweden.

She also received recognition from well-known public figures. Among those who publicly supported Alexievich were – to name just a few: Jury Ziser, owner of Tut.by, Belarus's most popular online news service, the writer and politician Uladzimir Niakliajeŭ, the former presidential candidate Sannikaŭ, who wrote an article about Alexievich in *The Guardian*, as well as representatives of the business community, including the chairman of Belgazprombank Viktar Babaryka. An opinion poll showed that 57 per cent of Belarusian respondents saw the Nobel Prize as 'a source of pride and international recognition of Alexievich's talent' (IISEPS 2015b).

This impressive number suggests a high level of recognition for Alexievich's award and its significance for society at large, despite the politically sensitive nature of Alexievich's works and the critical stance of the authorities towards the writer's public activity. At the same time, however, the remaining 43 per cent of the respondents saw things differently; almost 10 per cent of them assessed the presentation of the Nobel Prize in Literature to Alexievich as 'an attempt by the West to harm Belarus and Russia'. Interestingly, the Belarusian community was divided over the question of whether Alexievich should be praised and recognised as a Belarusian writer.

## The Diffusion of Nationalist Sentiment in the Post-Soviet Space

The issue of Alexievich's national identity came to the forefront of public discussions together with the proliferation of nationalist sentiment across the post-Soviet space. The rise of nationalist consciousness in Belarus was instigated by growing nationalism in Russia in the wake of the Ukrainian crisis that started in November 2013 with Euromaidan and led to the annexation of Crimea by Russia and military actions in southern and eastern Ukraine. The diffused elements of Russian nationalism were adapted by the Belarusian community to fit local conditions. As a result, the number of Belarusians who preferred independence, as opposed to both European and Eurasian integration projects, and valued the stability and independence of Belarus has been growing (see Kryvoi and Wilson 2015; IISEPS 2015a). Alongside these trends, the Belarusian authorities have started to promote national identity and unity. Thus, several steps have been taken to promote the Belarusian language (Barushka 2015), and Lukashenka has intermittently underlined the fact that Belarus is not a part of the Russian world, but an independent country (see, for instance, Kryvoi and Wilson 2015; Bohdan 2015; The official internet portal of the President of the Republic of Belarus 2015a; Lukashenka 2015a). The attitudes of the general public in Belarus to Alexievich's Nobel Prize reflect an increasing diffusion of nationalist sentiment in the post-Soviet region.

### The 'Belarusianness' of Alexievich

Besides the question of the literary quality of her prose, the 'Belarusianness' of Alexievich has become one of the main subjects of critique in both Belarus and Russia. Belarusian critics could not but recall a provocative statement Alexievich made in Germany in June 2013, after her receipt of the Peace Prize of the German Publishers and Booksellers Association. In an interview with the German daily *Frankfurter Allgemeine Zeitung*, she stated that the Belarusian language is 'rural and literarily unripe' (Holm 2013). This caused a wave of protest in the Belarusian media and on social networks. Subsequent statements made by Alexievich in an attempt to explain her position in more detail were even more confusing and cast 'a shadow on the judgment of the famous writer' (Lashuk 2013).

Now, two years later, Alexievich has again been denounced for her attitude towards the Belarusian language and the insufficient attention she affords Belarus. For example, the newspaper *Naša Niva* published an article with some statistics on the words used in Alexievich's Nobel lecture, according to which the word 'Belarus' was only used six times, whereas the word 'Russian' was used twenty times (2015). The view that Belarusian literature should be written in Belarusian has been expressed by organisations such as the civic campaign Budźma and the Belarusian Solidarity Platform. The internet community *by_mova* even conducted a poll on whether Alexievich can truly be considered a Belarusian writer (Charnysh 2015a). A number of political figures, such as Zmicier Daškievič, a leader of the opposition movement, and writers such as Sviatlana Kurs and Adam Hlobus, have expressed their concerns about Alexievich's writing in Russian (see, for instance, Charnysh 2015b; Berezyuk and others 2015).

### Alexievich and the Russian World

Considering Alexievich's works and awards through a prism of national identity was also characteristic of Russian public figures and mass media. Here two main trends representing two different worlds permeated by nationalist sentiment can be observed. First, some commentators suggested that Alexievich had become a representative of the Russian World and could become a significant inspirational figure (Kashin 2015; Gelman 2015). To explain: the 'Russian World' alluded to here is a conceptual construct outside the domain of official discourse, the current political order, and conspiracy theories, and closer to the opposition, the critical electorate, and the liberal intelligentsia.

As Russian writer and critic Bykov put it, it is 'not the Russian World that we keep hearing about on TV – not the world of aggression, lies and chauvinism – but the world of the struggle for truth, a world of kindness and humanness' (2015). These views to a certain extent reflect those of Alexievich, who distances herself from the Soviet and current Russian political authorities, stating: 'I love a good Russian world, a humanitarian Russian world, a world which is respected by the whole world – the literature, the ballet, the great music. Yes, I love this world. But I do not love the world of Beria, Stalin, Putin, Shoigu – it's not my world' (2015a). Herewith she points out the deep dividing line between society and the authorities, which still exists in the post-Soviet space even after the collapse of the USSR, and reveals the alienation of autocratic authorities from society.

The discourse of a different set of Russian commentators also concentrated on the Russian World, this time contingent on Putin and strong power. Thus, some public figures, like the nationalist writer Zakhar Prilepin, saw the awarding of the Nobel Prize to Alexievich as a sign of acceptance of Russia's power and significance (2015). Yuri Polyakov, editor of the Russian weekly *Literaturnaya Gazeta*, stated: 'It's a purely political act. The Nobel Prize in Literature has no relation to literature, it exists as an award to support oppositional writers. The political component comes increasingly to the fore' (Hansegard and others 2015).

Critics cited the anti-Sovietism of Alexievich and accused her of inciting hatred against Russia. Even though the coverage of Alexievich's prize in the Russian state media wasn't 'comparable to the bullying campaign against Pasternak and Solzhenitsyn' after they received their Nobel Prizes, state journalists wrote according to a recognisable pattern, adapted from their Soviet forerunners (Drakokhrust 2015). To start with, some article titles were written in dry and pompous language, with examples like: 'The buzz of the reactionist propaganda around the literary weed' from the Soviet *Prauda* (Zaslavskij 1958) or 'A literary woman of the right calibre' from the Russian *Literaturnaya Gazeta* (Puhnavzev 2015).

Furthermore, the way the state media in Russia criticised Alexievich sometimes amounted to ideologically loaded shaming. The content of the articles usually covered the following thematic areas: The West as an enemy, the critical stance of the author towards authorities and national history, and the poor quality of the literary work under consideration. Thus, the Russian newspaper *Kultura* described a plot, according to which the Nobel prize was awarded to a Belarusian writer criticising the Soviet past and Russian authorities in order to discredit Putin and instigate public protests (Ivanov 2015).

The suggestions that Alexievich acted as a Western political agent and promoted anti-Soviet sentiments were exploited in many articles from the state media, including *Literaturnaya Gazeta* (Puhnavzev 2015) and *Komsomolskaya Pravda* (Grishin 2015). All in all, the assessments Alexievich received from this group of commentators was revealing of the current vision of world affairs popular among the political elites in Russia. In order to strengthen national identity and legitimise the domestic autocratic regime, the authorities appeal to national memory and instrumentalise nationalist sentiments throughout society.

## Multiple Identities, Time and Space

Retrospectively, Alexievich's award of the Nobel Prize in Literature involved active discussion, marked by polarised opinions and politically loaded criticism, in a number of countries. It deepened divisions between various interconnected opposites, such as the authorities and the opposition, the authorities and society, Belarusian and Russian identities, and the Soviet past and the post-Soviet present. At the same time, Alexievich, perhaps deliberately, neither evoked solidarity among any group of like-minded people, nor united any political or social force.

Having realised that Alexievich would not promote a positive image of official Belarus internationally, the Belarusian authorities attempted to underplay the significance of the Nobel Prize. Although her works, which were removed from the school curriculum in the early 2000s, will be re-integrated in the basic programme (tut.by 2015a), Alexievich is not considered by the authorities to be a loyal intellectual or a public figure capable of contributing to the legitimisation of the regime domestically or internationally. Accordingly, officials continue to pursue a strategy of disregarding her writings and her acknowledged status as a distinguished writer. Russian authorities have largely ignored Alexievich's success.

At the same time, both the choice of the Nobel Committee and Alexievich's insufficiently critical behaviour towards the autocratic regime in Belarus left the opposition in Belarus unsatisfied. Despite Alexievich's accusatory statements regarding the USSR and autocratic regimes in Belarus and Russia, as well the latter's intervention in Ukraine, she has not become a voice for the opposition, to a large extent owing to her independent and non-radical attitude to politics. In response to criticism of her Nobel Lecture from the oppositional Belarusian community, which reproached her for not highlighting the current political situation in Belarus, she noted that writers 'should not make a rally of their Nobel lecture. [...] I have said everything, but as a writer' (Belsat 2015b). Alexievich used part of her Nobel Prize winnings to purchase an apartment in a gigantic, oligarch-funded building which to many Belarusians is a symbol of the arbitrariness and permissiveness of the autocracy. This points to Alexievich's unwillingness to become a moral authority (tut.by 2015b).

When making political statements, she often philosophically and insightfully recourses to history and social phenomena. Thus, commenting on the current political situation in Russia, she explains:

> there is a collective Putin, consisting of some millions of people who
> do not want to be humiliated by the West [...] There is a little piece
> of Putin in everyone (Donadio 2016).

When being asked about her political vision of Belarus, she admitted that she is against revolution and pleaded for the invention of a Belarusian Gandhism in order to undertake necessary reforms (Alexievich 2015a). Her reference to Gandhism, signifying that she is against violent and immediate change in political power and prefers non-violent resistance and gradual peaceful reforms, once again exemplified Alexievich's measured approach to politics.

Alexievich has also faced considerable criticism and mistrust from the broad public in both Belarus and Russia because of the nationalist mood prevailing in these societies, especially since the beginning of the Ukrainian crisis. Alexievich's multiple identities and her critical stance towards the Soviet regime confuse those who actively appeal to historical continuity in their search for national identity in Belarus and Russia. Belarusian nationalists stress that by writing in Russian, Alexievich lays claim to a global – rather than Belarusian - identity and has failed to properly address the autocratic regime in Belarus during her appearances in Stockholm. Her critics in Russia complain that her books portray life in the USSR in an unfavourable light and thereby undermine the very foundation of the new Russian nationalism. There is also another country which has played a role in shaping Alexievich's identity: Ukraine, where she was born and where her win was received mostly positively (Charnysh 2015b). Thus, in her Nobel lecture, Alexievich told those listening:

> I have three homes: my Belarusian land, the homeland of my father,
> where I have lived my whole life; Ukraine, the homeland of my
> mother, where I was born; and Russia's great culture, without which
> I cannot imagine myself. All are very dear to me (Alexievich 2015b).

The perception of Alexievich's works and the reactions to her Nobel Prize are influenced by the processes of authoritarian learning across space and time. Within the spatial dimension, all three countries to which Alexievich is connected are neighbours, and consequently often face a spillover effect with regards to the diffusion of policies, norms and practices. In the last decade, and especially since the beginning of the crisis in Ukraine and the increasing confrontation between Russia and the West, playing the nationalist card and striving to crystallise and define national identity have been characteristic of the political and cultural landscape in all three countries. Given these circumstances, Alexevich's Nobel Prize has been predominantly considered in the context of growing nationalism. Despite the attempts of Russia, Belarus and Ukraine to stress the uniqueness of each of their own national identities, 'the passage from Soviet state to national state was experienced by them all' (Snyder 2015). Thus, the temporal dimension connects the Soviet past and post-Soviet present, making both Russia and Belarus 'nostalgic dictatorships' (Snyder 2015). Paradoxically, official Soviet nostalgia and collective Soviet memory to a large extent define the perception of Alexievich's texts about the Soviet past and the Soviet Person, the Red Man, in Belarusian and Russian societies.

Alexievich could contribute to the strengthening of national identity in Belarus and Russia with her critical approach to historical consciousness and collective memory in the post-Soviet space. Nevertheless, her writings about the Soviet past and the following transitional period, which constitute 'a monument to suffering and courage in our time', according to the Swedish Academy, and which denunciate political regimes in the USSR and in post-Soviet countries, have led to her marginalisation by the current authorities in Belarus and Russia (The official web site of the Nobel Prize, n.d.). At the same time, because of Alexievich's multifaceted identity, it would be difficult for her to use her Nobel Prize to inspire and mobilise the opposition and critical public in either country due to the increasing nationalism and desire for self-determination in the region. All this prevents Alexievich from becoming a unifying figure for the post-Soviet community.

## Conclusion

This article analysed how the unintended impact of autocratic learning from the past and diffusion of norms and practices among neighbouring states influences official policies and public moods. It explained the reactions in Belarus and Russia to the awarding of the Nobel Prize in Literature to Svetlana Alexievich in 2015 by pointing out the interconnection between the common Soviet past of these countries and the spread of nationalist sentiments in the post-Soviet space following the Ukrainian crisis. The study showed that Alexievich's dismissal of autocratic regimes and her multifaceted identity, which encompasses Soviet, Russian, Belarusian and Ukrainian elements, prevent her from becoming a unifying figure in the post-Soviet countries.

While this contribution mainly discussed the unintended consequences of external influences, some scholars claim that political actors can intentionally use the unintended impact of their policies to achieve certain objectives (see, for example, Casier 2015). In the case of Alexievich's Nobel Prize, it would be interesting to look in more detail at how and for what purpose individual politicians or political groups have attempted to manage the situation surrounding the win. It would also be worthwhile to compare the treatment of disloyal intellectuals by autocratic regimes in other regions of the world to explore both commonalities and specific features in the approaches of individual countries or groups of countries. These suggestions could be used to inform the future research agenda in autocracy studies.

### References

Alexievich, S., 2015a. Available at: <https://baj.by/en/content/hour-after-nobel-full-text-sviatlana-alexievichs-press-conference>, [Accessed 2 February 2016].

Alexievich, S., 2015b. Nobel Lecture, Available at: <https://www.nobelprize.org/nobel_prizes/literature/laureates/2015/alexievich-lecture_en.html>, [Accessed 23 March 2016].

Alexievich, S., 2015c. Banquet Speech. Available at: <https://www.nobelprize.org/nobel_prizes/literature/laureates/2015/alexievich-speech_en.html>, [Accessed 23 March 2016].

Ambrosio, T., 2013. Authoritarian Belarus between Russia and Europe, in R. Vanderhill, and M. E. Alerpete Jr. eds., *International Dimensions of Authoritarian Persistence: Lesson from Post-Soviet States,* Lanham: Lexington Books, pp. 193-217.

Barushka, K., 2015. After decades of Russian dominance, Belarus begins to reclaim its language. Available at: <http://www.theguardian.com/world/2015/jan/28/-sp-russian-belarus-reclaims-language-belarusian>, [Accessed 20 March 2016].

Belarus Segodnya, 2015. Svetlana Alexievich: 'Pravdu nuzhno podavat', kak ona est". Available at: <http://www.sb.by/kultura/news/svetlana-aleksievich-pravdu-nuzhno-davat-kak-ona-est.html>, [Accessed 20 March 2016].

Belaruspartisan, 2015. 'Sviatkujem Nobielia razam!' Available at: <http://www.belaruspartisan.org/life/326340/>, [Accessed 20 April 2016].

Belsat, 2015a. Lukashenka: hardly had Alexievich got Nobel Prize when she threw mud on country. Available at: <http://belsat.eu/en/news/lukashenka-

pra-aleksievich-ne-paspela-atrymats-nobelya-a-uzho-vylila-brud-na-krainu/>, [Accessed 20 April 2016].

Belsat, 2015b. One should not make rally of Nobel lecture – Svetlana. Available at: <http://belsat.eu/en/news/one-should-not-make-rally-of-nobel-lecture-svetlana-alexievich/>, [Accessed 01 September 2016].

Berezyuk, E., Kostyukevich, N., and Inanez, S., 2015. 'Svetlana - proekt iskliuchitel'no samoi sebia'. Kak otreagirovali deiateli kul'tury na pobedu Aleksievich. Available at: <http://news.tut.by/society/467784.html>, [Accessed 14 April 2016].

Bohdan, S., 2015. Is Lukashenka preparing for a war? Available at: <http://belarusdigest.com/story/lukashenka-preparing-war-21232>, [Accessed 14 April 2016].

Brooks, X., 2015. Available at: <https://twitter.com/xanbrooks/status/652077445554794497>, [Accessed 04 January 2016].

Bykov, D., 2015. O prisuzhdenii Svetlane Aleksievich Nobelevskoi premii po literature. Available at: <http://echo.msk.ru/programs/beseda/1636786-echo/>, [Accessed 24 March 2016].

Casier, T., 2015. National Level: How the EU and Russia Manage Their Unintended Impact on Their Common Neighbours, in A. Obydenkova, and A. Libman eds., *Autocratic and Democratic External Influences in Post-Soviet Eurasia,* Farnham: Ashgate, pp. 89 – 107.

Charnysh, V., 2015a. Prisoners of authoritarianism: Alexievich and her critic. Available at: <http://belarusdigest.com/story/prisoners-authoritarianism-alexievich-and-her-critics-15749>, [Accessed 04 March 2016].

Charnysh, V., 2015b. Belarus, Ukraine, Russia react to Alexievich's Nobel Prize. Available at: <http://belarusdigest.com/story/belarus-ukraine-russia-react-alexievich%E2%80%99s-nobel-prize-23465>, [Accessed 04 April 2016].

Charter97.org, 2015. Svetlana Alexievich: 'Putin now lives inside every Russian'. Available at: <https://charter97.org/en/news/2015/5/15/151651/>, [Accessed 12 May 2016].

Deutsche Welle, 2015. Belarus literature Nobel winner Alexievich warns of 'soft dictatorship'. Available at: <http://www.dw.com/en/belarus-literature-nobel-winner-alexievich-warns-of-soft-dictatorship/a-18775046>, [Accessed 2 May 2016].

Donadio, R., 2016. Svetlana Alexievich, Nobel Laureate of Russian misery, has an English-language milestone. Available at: <http://www.nytimes.com/2016/05/21/books/svetlana-alexievich-a-nobel-laureate-of-russian-misery-has-her-english-debut.html>, [Accessed 21 May 2016].

Drakachrust, Y., 2015. December 2015: Paradoxes of Belarusian love to Alexievich. Available at: <http://www.iiseps.org/?p=3898&lang=en>, [Accessed 24 March 2016].

Erdmann, G., Bank, A., Hoffmann, B., and Richter, T., 2013. International Cooperation of Authoritarian Regimes: toward a Conceptual Framework, Working Paper 229, Hamburg, GIGA.

Gelman, M., 2015. Available at: <https://twitter.com/galerist/status/652096256639156224?ref_src=twsrc%5Etfw>, [Accessed 21 March 2016].

Gessen, M., 2015. The memory keeper. Available at: <http://www.newyorker.com/magazine/2015/10/26/the-memory-keeper>, [Accessed 2 April 2016].

Govoritmoskva, 2015. Aleksievich ne soglasilas' s kritikoi Lukashenko. Available at: <http://govoritmoskva.ru/news/56791/>, [Accessed 2 May 2016].

Grishin, A., 2015. Zhenskoie li litso u Svetlany Aleksievich? Available at: <http://www.kp.ru/daily/26443/3314068>, [Accessed 14 April 2016].

Hansegard, J., Maloney, J., and Marson, J., 2015. Nobel Prize in Literature awarded to Svetlana Alexievich. Available at: <http://www.wsj.com/articles/nobel-prize-for-literature-awarded-to-svetlana-alexievich-1444304784>, [Accessed 25 May 2016].

Heydemann, S., and Leenders, R., 2011. Authoritarian Learning and Authoritarian Resilience: Regime Responses to the 'Arab Awakening', *Globalizations*, 8 (5), pp. 647-53.

Holm, K., 2013. Uns fehlt die Kultur des Glücks. Available at: <http://www.faz.net/aktuell/feuilleton/bilder-und-zeiten/ein-gespraech-mit-der-friedenspreistraegerin-swetlana-alexijewitsch-uns-fehlt-die-kultur-des-gluecks-12238217.html>, [Accessed 9 April 2016].

Hulpachova, M., 2015. Belarus bookshop braves the state to publish Nobel winner's work. Available at: <http://www.theguardian.com/world/2015/oct/19/svetlana-alexievich-nobel-belarus>, [Accessed 2 March 2016].

IISEPS, 2015a. IISEPS news, 1(75). Available at: <http://www.iiseps.org/?p=1333&lang=en>, [Accessed 4 April 2016].

IISEPS, 2015b. Results of the nation opinion poll conducted on December 2-12, 2015. Available at: <http://www.iiseps.org/?p=3919&lang=en>, [Accessed 4 April 2016].

Ivanov, G., 2015. Zarubezhnye eksperty: 'Aleksievich prosto vypolniaet zadanie Zapada'. Available at: <http://portal-kultura.ru/articles/best/122813-

zarubezhnye-eksperty-aleksievich-prosto-vypolnyaet-zadanie-zapada/>, [Accessed 24 March 2016].

Kalesnikava, M., 2015. Lukashenka orders to present Alexievich's books to Swedish Ambassador. Available at: <http://euroradio.fm/en/lukashenka-orders-present-alexievichs-books-swedish-ambassador>, [Accessed 15 May 2016].

Kashin, O., 2015. Lider nastoiashchego russkogo mira: kem mogla by stat' Svetlana Aleksievich. Available at: <https://slon.ru/posts/57652>, [Accessed 21 March 2016].

Kasmach, L., 2016. 'Second-Hand' coverage: Alexievich's Nobel Prize in the Belarus' media. Available at: <http://belarusdigest.com/story/%E2%80%9Csecond-hand%E2%80%9D-coverage-alexievichs-nobel-prize-belarus-media-24242>, [Accessed 04 March 2016].

Kryvoi, Y., and Wilson, A., 2015. From Sanctions to Summits: Belarus after the Ukraine Crisis. ECFR Policy Memo 132. Available at: <http://www.ecfr.eu/page/-/ECFR_132_Belarus_(May_5_-_version_2).pdf>, [Accessed 4 April 2016].

Kuchta, P., 2015. Culmination. People in the airport welcomed Sviatlana Alexievich with flowers and books. Available at: <http://en.eurobelarus.info/news/society/2015/12/17/culmination-people-in-the-airport-welcomed-sviatlana-alexievich.html>, [Accessed 1 April 2016].

Lankina, T., Libman, A, and Obydenkova, A., 2016. Authoritarian and Democratic Diffusion, *Comparative Political Studies*, pp. 1-31.

Lashuk, N., 2013. Svetlana Alexievich: Belarusian language is rural and literary unripe. Available at: <http://belarusdigest.com/story/svetlana-alexievich-belarusian-language-rural-and-literary-unripe-14532>, [Accessed 20 April 2016].

Leenders, R., 2016. Arab Regimes' International Linkages and Authoritarian Learning: toward an Ethnography of Counter-Revolutionary Bricolage. A memo for the workshop 'International Diffusion and Cooperation of Authoritarian Regimes', held on June 8-9, 2016 in Hamburg, Germany.

Lukashenka, A., 2015a. Available at: <http://president.gov.by/ru/news_ru/view/obraschenie-s-poslaniem-k-belorusskomu-narodu-i-natsionalnomu-sobraniju-11301/>, [Accessed 14 May 2016].

Lukashenka, 2015b. Available at: <http://www.sb.by/en-belarus-magazine/economy-2/article/energy-for-the-future-3-11.html>, [Accessed 15 May 2016].

McFaul, M., Magen A., and Stoner-Weiss, K., 2009. Evaluating International Influences on Democratic Transitions: Research Guide for Case Study Authors, Center on Democracy, Development and the Rule of Law: Stanford. Available at:

<http://fsi.stanford.edu/events/evaluating_international_influences_on_democratic_development__authors_workshop>, [Accessed 2 August 2013].

Melnykovska, I., Plamper, H., and Schweickert, R., 2012. Do Russia and China Promote Autocracy in Central Asia? *Asia Europe Journal,* 10 (1), pp. 75-89.

Naša Niva, 2013. Jakija slovy najčasciej hučali ŭ Nobielieŭskaj lekcyi Aleksijevič? Available at: <http://nn.by/?c=ar&i=161353>, [Accessed 21 April 2016].

Obydenkova, A., and Libman, A., eds. *Autocratic and democratic external influences in post-Soviet Eurasia,* Farnham: Ashgate

Prilepin, Z., 2015. Svetlana Rossii! Available at: <http://izvestia.ru/news/592832>, [Accessed 25 March 2016].

Puhnavzev, O., 2015. Literator nuzhnogo kalibra. Available at: <http://lgz.ru/article/-40-6528-14-10-2015/literator-nuzhnogo-kalibra/>, [Accessed 24 March 2016].

Silitski, V., 2010. Survival of the Fittest: Domestic and International Dimension of the Authoritarian Reaction in the Former Soviet Union Following the Colored Revolution, *Communist and Post-Communist Studies,* 43 (4), pp. 339-50.

Snyder, T., 2015. Svetlana Alexievich: the truth in many voices. Available at: <http://www.nybooks.com/daily/2015/10/12/svetlana-alexievich-truth-many-voices/>, [Accessed 2 May 2016].

The official internet portal of the President of the Republic of Belarus, 2015a. Stenogramma vstrechi s predstavitelyami belorusskih i zarubeznih SMI. Available at: <http://president.gov.by/ru/news_ru/view/stenogramma-vstrechi-s-predstaviteljami-belorusskix-i-zarubezhnyx-smi-10760/>, [Accessed 11 May 2016].

The official internet portal of the President of the Republic of Belarus, 2015b. Alexander Lukashenka sends greetings to Nobel Literature Prize winner Svetlana Alexievich. Available at: <http://president.gov.by/en/news_en/view/alexander-Lukashenka-sends-greetings-to-nobel-literature-prize-winner-svetlana-alexievich-12293/>, [Accessed 15 May 2016].

The official web site of the Nobel Prize, n.d. Svetlana Alexievich - Facts. Available at: <https://www.nobelprize.org/nobel_prizes/literature/laureates/2015/alexievich-facts.html>, [Accessed 28 May 2016].

Tut.by, 2015a. So sleduiushchego goda v shkolnykh programmakh poiaviatsia proizvedenia Svetlany Aleksievich. Available at: <http://news.tut.by/society/467935.html>, [Accessed 19 May 2016].

Tut.by, 2015b. Svetlana Aleksievich kupila kvartiru v dome Chizha i dereviannuiu dachiu v Silichakh. Available at: <http://news.tut.by/society/495336. html>, [Accessed 19 May 2016].

Ukraine Today, 2015. Nobel laureate Alexievich holds press conference in Berlin. Available at: <http://uatoday.tv/society/nobel-laureate-alexievich-holds-press-conference-in-berlin-510937.html>, [Accessed 15 May 2016].

Vanderhill, R., 2012. *Promoting Authoritarianism Abroad*, Boulder: Lynne Rienner.

Zaslavskii, D., 1958. Shumikha reakcionnoi propagandy vokrug literaturnogo sorniaka, *Pravda*, No. 299 (14693), p.4.

# World War II Criminals in Belarusian Internet Mass-Media: The Cases of Anthony Sawoniuk and Vladimir Katriuk

BY

VERANIKA LAPUTSKA[1]

Jews have been an important component of multicultural society on the territory of Belarus for many centuries. At the beginning of the 20th century, they were also becoming increasingly involved in politics, forming several specifically Jewish parties and becoming members of many other emerging political parties in the Russian empire. After the Bolshevik revolution, they continued to play an important role in the development of Belarusian culture and science. According to data from the Jewish Community in Belarus, around 407,000 Jews lived on Belarusian territory in 1926 (Evreiskaia obshina v Resublike Belarus', 2004).

The 1939 a Soviet census recorded 375,092 Jews living on the territory of Soviet Belarus before its unification with Western Belarus (Vsesoiuznaia perepis' naseleniia 1939). A Polish census from 1931 reported that 283,300 Jews were living in Western Belarus, then part of Poland (Katljarchuk 2013, p. 13). Overall, around 658,400 Jews inhabited Soviet Belarusian territories by June 1941 when Nazi Germany attacked the Soviet Union. Later, this figure would increase by thousands, as up to 820,000 Jewish migrants from occupied Poland poured over the border (Katljarchuk 2013, p. 13). The vast majority of them were killed during 1941 – 1945 as a result of the Holocaust. No more than 10 – 12% of the Jewish population in Western Belarus, and 50% in Central or Eastern Belarus, survived World War II; overall, approximately 800,000 Jews were liquidated on the territory of occupied Belarus (Rudling 2013b, p. 121). In fact, the USSR census of 1959 stated that only 150,084 Jews were living in Belarus at that time (Vsesoiuznaia perepis' naseleniia 1959).

Not only did the Holocaust physically eliminate Jews from the territory of Belarus, it also seems to have erased their presence from the collective memory

[1] The author expresses her deep gratitude to Dist. Prof. David R. Marples and Prof. Annamaria Orla-Bukowska for their valuable assistance and advice on the research; Aliaksandr Herasimenka for his help on acquiring information from the British Library; Prof. Yaraslau Kryvoi and three anonymous peer-reviewers for their helpful comments and suggestions.

of the Soviet population. Thus, in its public rhetoric, the Soviet Union usually sublimated 'the genocide of Jews within the massive overall human losses suffered by all peoples' of the USSR during World War II (Dean 2010, p. 267). Research devoted to the Holocaust was a 'taboo' topic for Soviet scholarship until 1988 (Rudling 2013a, p. 61), and school textbooks began referring to this terrible episode of human history only in the late era of the Soviet Union[2].

Attitudes towards this issue have not changed greatly since Belarus gained its independence. The cult of the 'Great Patriotic War' and the heroism of Belarusian partisans are key elements of official state propaganda, whereas the Holocaust is very much neglected by Belarusian authorities, who are wary that competing narratives could overshadow their main nation-building myth. The Belarusian state tries not to attract too much attention to the small Jewish community existing on its territory today, although gradual positive changes are taking place.

Thus, several Jewish cultural and historical museums do exist in Belarus, some synagogues are being renovated, and many monuments to the Jewish victims of World War II have been erected in Belarusian towns and cities with the support of the state (Katljarchuk 2013, pp. 16-17)[3]. However, according to the Simon Wiesenthal Center, Belarus remains one of the least active countries in investigating the former Nazi executioners who murdered Jews on Belarusian territory; it is consistently ranked 'X', for countries that fail to provide pertinent data on Nazi war criminals (Wiesenthal Center Annual Report 2013 and Wiesenthal Center Annual Report 2014). As a result, Belarusian public discourse is not very active in openly discussing the Holocaust or the activities of Nazi collaborators who participated in the 'Final Solution' on Belarusian territory.

The aim of this paper is to describe the Belarusian Internet mass-media discourses surrounding the cases of two Nazi World War II criminals: Anthony Sawoniuk (who changed his name from Andrei when he moved to the United Kingdom) and Vladimir Katriuk. Anthony Sawoniuk, a citizen of the United Kingdom, was born in the Belarusian town of Damačava (or Domachevo in Russian transliteration), where he allegedly participated in the massacre of the local Jewish population. He was prosecuted in London and found guilty. Vladimir Katriuk, a Ukrainian-born citizen of Canada, was a soldier in the *Schutzmannschaft Bataillon 118* during

---

[2] For more on Holocaust memory politics in the BSSR and then in Belarus since 1991 see A. Katljarchuk, 'World War II Memory Politics: Jewish, Polish and Roma Minorities of Belarus', The Journal of Belarusian Studies, 2013:1, pp. 14 – 18; P.A. Rudling, 'The Invisible Genocide: The Holocaust in Belarus', in *Bringing the Dark Past to Light*, ed. J. – P. Himka and J. B. Michlic, University of Nebraska Press, 2013, pp. 59 – 82; P. A. Rudling, 'Neprykmietny hienacyd: Chalakost u Bielarusi'. *ARCHE 2, July 2013*, pp. 124 – 138.

[3] Nevertheless, only one wall in hall number 6 of the Museum of the History of the Great Patriotic War in Minsk is devoted to the Holocaust, and the total number of Jews killed on Belarusian territory is not specified, only the overall figure of civilians and prisoners of war murdered in Belarus during 1941 – 1945. The author visited the Museum on July 28, 2015.

WWII. During his time as a soldier, he allegedly perpetrated numerous atrocities on Belarusian territory (Rudling 2012, p. 42), including the Chatyń (Khatyn) massacre, where 149 Belarusians were killed.

FIGURE 1: The Belarusian Museum of the Great Patriotic War.
One of three stands devoted to the Holocaust in Belarus containing images
from Minsk and Viciebsk ghetto and a photo of victims killed in Viciebsk region.
Center-left inscription mentions a total number of Jews killed on the Belarusian
territory during Nazi occupation – between 500,000 and 800,000 people.
Photo taken by Veranika Laputska on 28 July 2015

This paper is obliged to use the term 'allegedly': despite the fact the Federal Court of Canada, during his denaturalization trail, established that as a member of Battalion 118 Mr Katriuk '[had taken part] in the operations in which his company was involved, and, as a result, was certainly engaged in fighting enemy partisans', Katrituk did not divulge that information when he immigrated to Canada. As a result, officially 'all deportation procedures were stopped in 2007 due to the lack of evidence'. Moreover, Mr Katriuk has never been tried solely for the Chatyń massacre.

Chatyń remains one of the most infamous tragedies to occur on Belarusian territory during World War II. It has become a symbol not only of Belarusian but also Soviet tragedy and grief caused by the Nazis (Chatyń Memorial Complex 2005 and Rudling 2012, pp. 29-58). After the war, the massacre was commemorated with a memorial complex located on the site of the former village of Chatyń near Minsk.

This paper aims to explore these two specific cases and compare their coverage in the Belarusian Internet mass-media, keeping in mind that in one case Belarusian Jews were massacred by an ethnic Belarusian, whereas in the second ethnic Belarusians were massacred by a non-Belarusian Nazi collaborator. The reason for investigating these cases in particular is the fact that both men were tried relatively recently (that is, the late 1990s – 2010s).

The article analyses the discourse among different groups of Belarusian Internet mass-media. Due to the overlap between the Russian and Belarusian Internet mass-media space, the paper also examines several Russian publications which have influenced information in the Belarusian media space. The study focuses on publications in three groups of web-sites:

1) state-owned and pro-government Internet mass-media. Such publications propagate the official opinions of the Belarusian authorities. This category includes the web-sites of the following Belarusian newspapers: *Belarus Segodnia – Sovetskaya Belorussiya, Respublika, Zviazda, Narodnaja Hazieta, Belorusskaya Niva, etc.;*

2) pro-democratic mass-media. These do not share the official views of the Belarusian state. They promote democratic values in Belarus and advocate freedom of speech. They include: Radio Free Europe/Radio Liberty (www.svaboda.org), *Belarusian Partisan* (www.belaruspartisan.org); European Radio for Belarus (euroradio.fm), *Naša Niva* (www.nn.by), *Charter 97* (www.charter97.org) and *Novy Čas* (www.novychas.info), etc.;

3) 'neutral' mass-media. Publications in this category refrain from promoting state ideology but also distance themselves from the opposition, thus lacking a particular political agenda. Such media also maintain a neutral attitude toward the Belarusian regime. They include: the news portal *Tut.by* (www.tut.by), *Vechernii Minsk* (vminsk. by), and the portals *naviny.by, udf.by, odsgomel.org* and *domachevo.com*, etc.

The paper analysed the Internet publications which garnered the most hits in a *Google* search of the cases in both Russian and Belarusian languages. Some additional information was also acquired in English when necessary. Thus, this study does not imply a comprehensive coverage of every article written on Sawoniuk and Katriuk on the Internet. Moreover, certain potentially relevant pieces may have already disappeared from the Internet due to the specific features of certain web-sites. A vast majority of websites only keep a certain amount of data – mainly depending on their age – so older pieces may have been deleted even from the cache.

Due to the fact that a well-elaborated methodology defining the political affiliation of Belarusian media outlets is missing, the author took the following criteria in mind when categorising Belarusian Internet mass-media according to the three groups described earlier: rhetoric and events described, language – Belarusian or Russian – where Belarusian media is more likely to be in opposition to the state, and the political and professional background of the journalists.

This paper consists of three parts. The first part describes the case of Anthony Sawoniuk and the subsequent reaction of Belarusian Internet mass-media both to the story itself and to the trial against him in London. The second part deals with the case of Vladimir Katriuk and academic and journalistic pieces written about him. It also explores the ways in which Belarusian and Russian media outlets presented Katriuk's story, as well as the interaction between Canada and the Russian Federation when the latter requested that Katriuk be extradited. The conclusion sums up the main discursive trends within each of the three groups of Internet mass-media and endeavours to explain the reasons behind the differences.

## Anthony (Andrei) Sawoniuk in Belarusian Internet Mass-Media

As Anne Applebaum stated in her 1999 article 'The nightmarish world that awaits a British jury,' published during the trial against Anthony Sawoniuk, the 'current [Belarusian] government has no interest in investigating either the nation's Nazi or its Soviet past...' (Applebaum 1999). The very poor coverage by the Belarusian media of the first and only Nazi war criminal prosecuted and convicted under the 1991 War Crimes Act in the United Kingdom proved the relevance of this citation. Several witnesses claimed that Sawoniuk personally killed several Jewish men and women in Nazi-occupied Damačava, his native town. Sawoniuk never pled guilty, despite the fact that the trial resulted in Sawoniuk receiving two life sentences for the murder of 18 Jews in Damačava (The Guardian 2005).

In 1999, the Minsk regional newspaper *Vechernii Minsk* published only one small piece regarding the case, which appeared in conjunction with data from the Belarusian Telegraph Agency – BelTA (Kobiak 1999). The article reported on the British jury delegation's visit to Damačava to investigate Sawoniuk's crimes and talk to the handful of surviving witnesses. It also discussed the 'few dozen journalists from leading Western countries, information agencies, and television companies' (Kobiak 1999). Belarusians journalists refrained from actively covering the event.

A Radio Liberty/Radio Free Europe journalist from Brest, Aleh Supruniuk, wrote an article regarding the trial of Mr Sawoniuk – also in 1999 (Supruniuk 1999). The article covered the British jury delegation's visit to Damačava and the story of Sawoniuk's accusations in the UK court.

FIGURE 2. Sawoniuk young.                FIGURE 3. Sawoniuk old.
Source: BBC 1999a                        Source: BBC 1999b

Another Belarusian pro-democratic website, *Naša Niva*, also devoted an article to Sawoniuk's case in 1999. The author of the article, journalist Valier Kalinoŭski, visited Damačava himself. He spoke with local inhabitants who still remembered Sawoniuk's crimes and described the town and what the execution site of the local Jewish population looked like in 1999 (Kalinoŭski 1999).

The website of the Institute of Human Rights in Moscow, www.hrights.ru, whose contributors include Belarusian historian and opposition activist Valiancin Holubieŭ, also mentioned the visit of the London court delegation to Brest and Damačava on 15–17 February 1999. The article was placed in a section covering Belarusian history and political and diplomatic relations between the Republic of Belarus and other countries, or more precisely, in the section covering relations between the UK and Belarus (Holubieŭ 1999). The publication pointed out that one of the reasons why Sawoniuk was not eligible for extradition to Belarus, the country where he was believed to have committed war crimes, was that the norms of the European Union's justice system forbid sending suspects to countries still practicing the death penalty.

Another series of articles devoted to Sawoniuk appeared after his death in a British prison in 2005. This time, not only the main opposition websites, such as *svaboda.org,* covered the story (Svaboda 2005), but so did the main state newspaper *Sovetskaia Belorussiia* (Krapivin, 2005). In a style very typical of state owned mass-media, which involves the use of slang expressions such as *na zone* (English 'in the zone', meaning 'in jail') or 'to give your soul to Devil' (as a description of Sawoniuk's death) (Krapivin 2005), the article explored the story of Sawoniuk's collaboration with the Nazis and his trial in the UK. This was the first time that an article regarding Anthony Sawoniuk appeared in a major Belarusian newspaper.

Notably, the author comments that Sawoniuk's real name, Andrei, was discovered the day before the article was written with the help of the Belarusian KGB.

A more detailed article by V. V. Datsyk about Sawoniuk appeared on the home page of his native town Damačava – *domachevo.com*, although it was probably uploaded later than his 1999 visit, as the website only began functioning in 2006 (Datsyk 2006). The article provides Sawoniuk's biography, confirming that he was born in Damačava and participated in the executions of people from his native town. It also contains several photographs, including one taken of the British jury delegation visiting Damačava. The author himself points out that he gathered the material from Wikipedia but also used several articles by British journalists published in 1999 in *The Independent* and *The Guardian* (Datsyk 2006).

Several Belarusian media outlets recalled Anthony (Andrei) Sawoniuk in 2010 when the Simon Wiesenthal Center placed another Nazi collaborator, Mikhail Gorshkow, on a list of the ten most wanted Nazi war criminals. Gorshkow was responsible for the murder of Jews in Sluck (Slutsk). The most popular Belarusian news portal – *tut.by* – described Sawoniuk in one article as 'the Damačava animal', due to his remarkable cruelty (Lashkevich 2010). The article listed five other Nazi war criminals persecuted in different countries for crimes committed on Belarusian territories during World War II.

FIGURE 4: The Belarusian Museum of the Great Patriotic War.
Installation devoted to Jewish victims of the World War II in Belarus. The third line in the centre states the number of Jews killed in Damačava in Brest region – 20,000.
Photo taken by Veranika Laputska on 28 July 2015

The fact that it was mainly 'neutral' and pro-democratic newspapers which published articles about Anthony Sawoniuk during his prosecution shows how little importance the Belarusian authorities placed on the topic of the Holocaust at that time. Despite the uniqueness of the trial against Sawoniuk, both for that particular time and for the judicial system of the United Kingdom, the Belarusian official media ignored the subject. The main state newspapers covered Sawoniuk's story only in 2005, when he died in a British jail in Norwich. Later on, his name re-emerged in the media after the discovery of other Nazi war criminals engaged in murders on Belarusian territory.

## Vladimir Katriuk in Belarusian Internet Mass-Media

Vladimir Katriuk was born in 1921 in the village of Luzhany near the city of Chernivtsi in Ukraine (Canada (Minister of Citizenship and Immigration) v. Katriuk 1999). After the start of the war between the Soviet Union and Nazi Germany, the latter organised two military formations out of the Organization of Ukrainian Nationalists (OUN): the Bandera wing (OUN(b)) and the Melnyk wing (OUN(m)). The Melnyk wing formed a 900-member Bukovinian Battalion (Bukovyns'kyi Kurin') and marched into Ukraine in summer 1941 (Rudling 2012, p. 34).

Katriuk was part of the Bukovinian Battalion and later the *Schutzmannschaft Bataillon 118*. As a member of *Bataillon 118*, Vladimir Katriuk fought in Ukraine, Belarus, East Prussia, and France. There he managed to join the French Foreign Legion, which he later deserted. Katriuk was able to acquire fake documents and stayed in France until August 1951, when he and his wife arrived in Quebec City under the name Schpirka after having obtained Canadian visas. Vladimir Katriuk did not tell the Canadian Consulate what he had been doing between 1938 and 1945. In 1957, both he and his wife changed their names to Katriuk and in 1958 they applied for Canadian Citizenship (Canada (Minister of Citizenship and Immigration) v. Katriuk, 1999).

Katriuk's name presumably came to light during the Deschenes Commission hearings in 1985-86. In the early 1980s, the Soviet KGB visited Katriuk's relatives in Ukraine; they later requested more information on him during the Gorbachev era. On 15 August 1996 Mrs and Mr Katriuk received a letter from the Ministry of Citizenship and Migration revoking their citizenship (Canada (Minister of Citizenship and Immigration) v. Katriuk 1999). In 1999, the Federal Court of Canada established that Mr Katriuk had gained access to Canada by providing false information. Nevertheless, denaturalization and deportation procedures were suspended in 2007 'due to lack of evidence' (Rudling 2012, p. 42).

FIGURE 5: Katriuk. Source: Pruitt 2015

The crimes of Vladimir Katriuk, which placed him third among the most wanted Nazi war criminals according to the Wiesenthal Center's 2014 annual report (Wiesenthal Center Annual Report 2014), re-emerged thanks to Swedish historian Per Anders Rudling (Rudling 2011, pp. 195 – 214). The name of Vladimir Katriuk had been mentioned previously during trials against Vasyl Meleshko[4] and Hryhoryi Vasiura, other members of *Schutzmannschaft Bataillon 118*, in 1975 and 1986 respectively (Rudling 2012, pp. 38 – 40). Both men were sentenced to capital punishment in a Soviet court. Vladimir Katriuk was never sued for his crimes (including the slaughter of the inhabitants of Chatyń in 1943) and died in Canada in 2015.

Chatyń was one of the numerous Belarusian towns and villages which was burned down, often along with their inhabitants, by the Nazis and their collaborators during World War II. Christian Gerlach states in his book *Kalkulierte Morde: Die deutsche Wirtschafts- und Vernichtungspolitik in Weißrußland* that massacres connected with the 'war against peasants' took place in 5,295 different locations in Belarus (Gerlach 1999, p. 943). Gerlach's analysis of Romanowski's statistics indicated that 3 per cent of these cases happened in 1941, 16 per cent in 1942, and 18 per cent in 1944, and no less than 63 per cent in 1943, when Chatyń's inhabitants were also massacred (Gerlach 1999, p. 943). The first half of 1943 coincided with the time when the Nazis had elaborated the notorious concept of 'dead zones' (Gerlach 1999, p. 1011)[5].

---

[4]  For more about Vasyl Meleshko see here: S.S. Maksimov, Istoriia odnogo predatelstva, *Neotvratimoie vozmezdiie: Po materialam sudebnykh protsessov nad izmennikami Rodiny, fashistkimi palachami i agentami imperialisticheskich razvedok*, Moskva, 1979, 294 p. *Voyennaya literatura.* Available at: <http://militera.lib.ru/h/sb_neotvratimoe_vozmezdie/12.html>. [Accessed 06.03.2016].

[5]  For more on various operations during that period in Belarus see Gerlach, 1999, pp. 1010 – 1036.

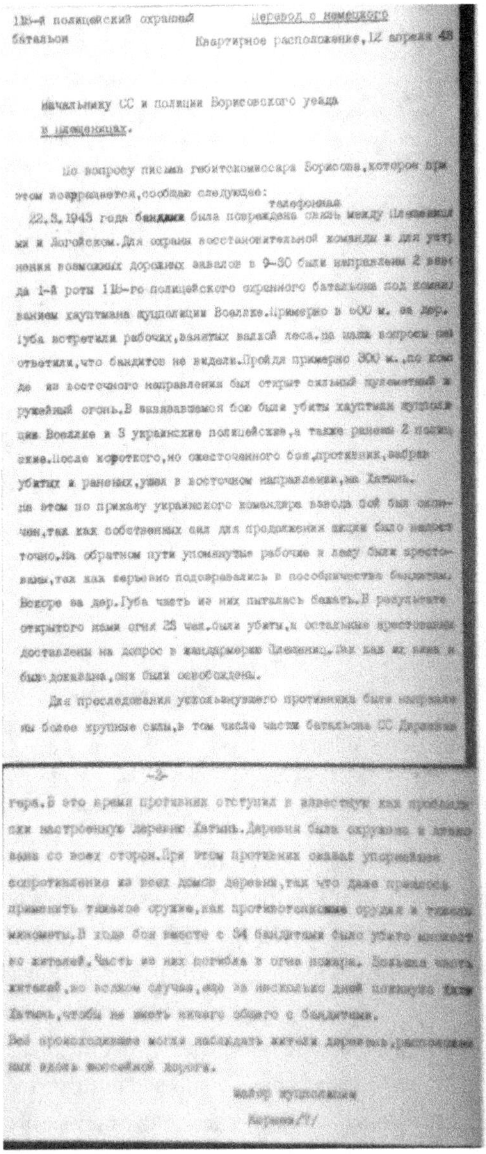

FIGURE 6: Chatyń museum. A photo of the report by *Schutzmannschaft Bataillon 118* about the Chatyń massacre translated into Russian. The document mentions participation of Ukrainian collaborators in the activities of *Schutzmannschaft Bataillon 118.* Photo taken by Veranika Laputska on 29 July 2015

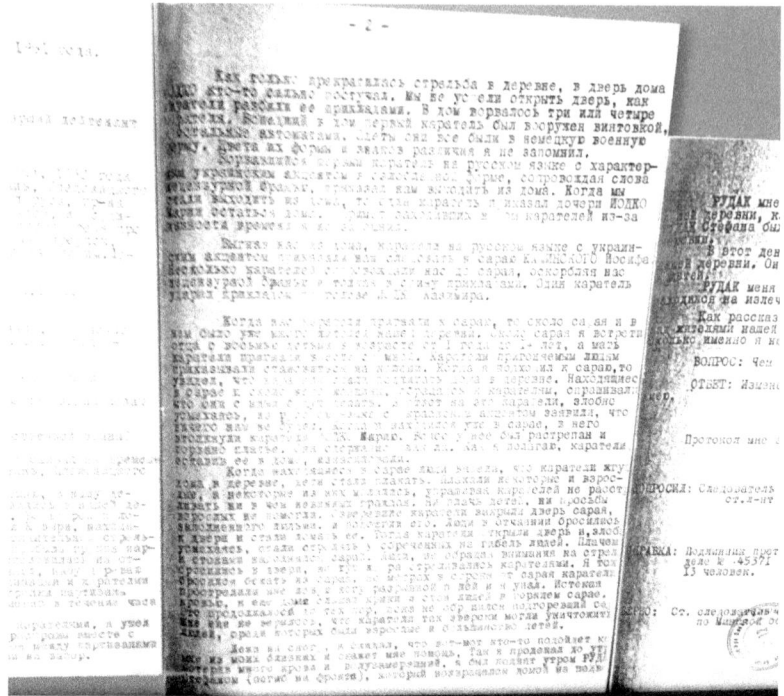

FIGURE 7: Chatyń museum. Evidence given by Anton Baranoŭski on 28 April 1961 confirming the *palicai* who executed the inhabitants of Chatyń spoke Russian with a strong Ukrainian accent. Anton Baranoúski witnessed the Chatyń massacre. Photo taken by Veranika Laputska on 29 July 2015

The Chatyń memorial became an important place for the commemoration of tragedies inflicted upon the Belarusian population during the war. BSSR officials opened the memorial complex in 1969 not far from Lahojsk in Minsk region. Since then, it has attracted tourists from many different countries[6]. Remarkably, the website of the memorial, which tells the story of the tragedy and describes the place of the Belarusian territories in Nazi policies, does not have a sub-section entitled 'Genocide of the Jews' or 'Genocide of the Roma[7]', Poles[8] or any other nationality also present in Belarus at the start of World War II.

The scale of their losses was also not reflected or mentioned on the territory of the monument itself (Katljarchuk 2013, p. 11). Instead, the website had a section entitled 'Genocide Policy,' whose sole sub-section was 'the Genocide of the Belarusian

---

[6] NB: during a short interview with Memorial's employees conducted by the author on 29 July 2015 they said that they were aware of Vladimir Katriuk's story. However, they added that they try not to mention too many executors in their oral and written narrative of the tragedy and skip using their last names in order to not to glorify them. Instead, guides try to tell the stories of those who survived. This should be the core of the story in their opinion.

[7] For more on the Roma Genocide see Katljarchuk, 2013, pp. 18 – 23.

[8] For more on the Genocide of the Polish minority, its history and politics in Belarus see *Ibidem*, pp. 23 – 29.

people', although according to international law the mass murders of the Belarusian civil population cannot be classified as genocide (Katljarchuk 2013, pp. 12 – 13).

FIGURE 8: Chatyń memorial. An iconic photo of the Chatyń sculpture of the Unconquered Man by S. Sielivanaú. It was based on Iosif Kaminski, a survivor of the tragedy who lost his family in fire. Photo taken by Veranika Laputska on 29 July 2015

FIGURE 9: Chatyń memorial. View on 'cemetery of villages' and the main monument. Photo taken by Veranika Laputska on 29 July 2015

FIGURE 10: Chatyń memorial. A monument stating how many Belarusians died
in 1941 – 1945 and how many villages, towns and cities were destroyed.
Photo taken by Veranika Laputska on 29 July 2015[9]

Notably, even though Per Anders Rudling's article clearly stated the involvement
of the *Schutzmannschaft Bataillon 118* in the extermination of the Jews on the
territories under its control, this part of Katriuk's biography was not covered by
the vast majority of Belarusian mass-media Internet publications. In contrast, the
mass-media from all three groups studied in this paper touched upon Vladimir
Katriuk's involvement in the Chatyń tragedy.

Thus, *Respublika,* the second largest state-owned Belarusian newspaper (after
*Sovetskaia Belorussiia*) published an article in April 2012 devoted to Vladimir
Katriuk's discovery in Canada (Respublika 2012). It described testimonies from
other members of the *Schutzmannschaft Bataillon 118,* revealing the details of the
Chatyń massacre using quite aggressive vocabulary.

Several news portals also covered this story. For instance, an article regarding
Katriuk's discovery appeared on the news portal *Naviny.by* (Naviny 2012). The
*Udf.by* news web-site published a similar article with a less neutral title (Udf.by
2012). In contrast to *Respublika* and *Naviny.by*, it avoided using words such as
'butcher'. A Homieĺ regional news web-site, *odsgomel.org,* also devoted some
space to news about one of the Chatyń executioners (Silnye novosti 2012).

Most opposition websites also mentioned Vladimir Katriuk's case in their
publications. *Naša Niva* reprinted a news item from the news agency *Interfax.by*
(Naša Niva 2012), as did the *Belarusian Partisan* web-site, which also published

---

[9] During a short interview with Memorial's employees conducted by the author on 29 July 2015 they
said they were aware of Vladimir Katriuk's recent story. However, they added they try not to mention
executors in their oral and written narrative of the tragedy and skip using their last names in order to
not to glorify them. That is why museum guides try to tell the stories of those who survived instead.

a story about Katriuk and Chatyń (Belaruspartisan 2012). *European Radio for Belarus* also devoted some space on their web-page to the topic (European Radio for Belarus 2012).

The story also attracted the attention of Belarus's neighbour Russia. One of the most important state channels – NTV – reported on Vladimir Katriuk from Canada in April 2012. Remarkably, the journalists pointed out that much attention was paid to the Chatyń massacre during the Soviet era in order to distract the world from the Katyn tragedy (NTV 2012). In 2015, in view of the conflict between Russia and Ukraine, it would be very unlikely for a Russian reportage to makes this claim, as Russian propaganda is becoming increasingly similar to Soviet reporting.

The story of the Chatyń massacre remains very important for the Belarusian public. Therefore, several more pieces worth mentioning have emerged on the Belarusian Internet since Vladimir Katriuk's story first broke. For example, in October 2013 the Belarusian state newspaper *Zviazda* published an article devoted to *Schutzmannschaft Bataillon 118* citing its other crimes, including the murder of Jewish families in Hrodna region in 1943 (Dalidovič and Marozava 2013). Hrodna University professor Sviatlana Marozava wrote the article together with Jauhien Dalidovič, a veteran of World War II and a former criminal investigator for the KGB in Hrodna region. The article mentioned that in many cases, in-depth research on Nazi crimes on Belarusian territory remains unlikely until the Belarusian KGB make secret files available to academics. At the moment, the self-induced isolation of the current Belarusian government, along with the lack of transparency and even secrecy of many of its institutions hamper scholarly activity in this field.

On 28 March 2014, a documentary film entitled *The Shameful Mystery of Khatyn*, filmed in 2008, was uploaded to *Youtube.com*. Interestingly, a note at the very end of the film states that it was made by a company named 'Super Reality' upon the request of the Joint Broadcasting System of the Russian Armed Forces.

At 22 minutes, the narrator shares the story of Vladimir Katriuk and his participation in the Chatyń massacre (Dykhovichnaia and Moloslavov 2008). What follows is a video shot during demonstrations by former members of the Ukrainian Insurgent Army and the Organisation of Ukrainian Nationalists (UIA/ OUN) in contemporary Ukraine. This is accompanied by the narrator's commentary on current Ukrainian memory politics. At minute 26, the narrator arrives at the Belarusian KGB special archive and enquires about Katriuk again (Dykhovichnaia and Moloslavov 2008). At minute 35, he reveals that Katriuk is an honorary citizen of Chernivtsi and shows several interviews with Chernivsti historians claiming that *Schutzmannschaft Bataillon 118* did not commit any crimes on Belarusian territory (Dykhovichnaia and Moloslavov 2008). At the end of the film, the narrator suggests that there might be other former members of *Schutzmannschaft Bataillon 118* still living in Ukraine.

The documentary clearly condemns not only members of *Schutzmannschaft Bataillon 118*, but also the Ukrainian memory politics adopted after the Orange Revolution. Remarkably, the film was uploaded on *youtube.com* in March 2014, in the midst of the Revolution of Dignity in Ukraine. The comments to the video have remained active in 2016 and contain hateful rhetoric against Ukrainians.

*Novy Čas* journalist Alieś Kirkievič conducted a sophisticated work of research in June 2014 which includes a digression into the history of Ukrainian collaborators and their activities on the Belarusian territories in World War II (Kirkievič 2014). He points out that this subject has become especially crucial for the Russian mass-media since the beginning of the Russian-Ukrainian conflict in 2014. According to him, Katriuk due to his origin[10] would continue to be a hot topic for both Russian and Belarusian state media as long as the conflict in Ukraine remains unresolved.

This hypothesis has proven true. Already on 17 June 2014, a documentary film entitled *Declassified History: Chatyń's Butchers*, produced by the Russian television channel *Rossiya – Kultura* (*Russia – Culture*), appeared on several popular video portals. The video, uploaded to *youtube.com,* had only comment– about Vladimir Katriuk's participation in the Chatyń massacre; Vladimir Katriuk was still alive at that time (Kuzovenkov 2014). None of the names of the rest of the 'butchers' appeared in the video description, even though there was only one reference to Katriuk in the entire film (Kuzovenkov 2014). The documentary film comprises part of a project called *Declassified History* and can be accessed together with other 'declassified' stories via the channel's webpage (Kuzovenkov 2014). The fact that Russian television (rather than Belarusian) decided to make a film about Chatyń and the people of Ukrainian origin who participated in the massacre there as late as 2014 remains suspicious, given Russian foreign policy towards Ukraine, as well as Ukraine's media image in Russia at the time.

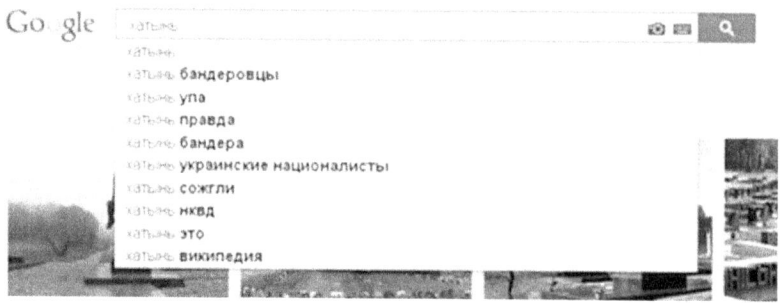

FIGURE 11: June 2014. Source: Kirkievič 2015

---

[10] NB: When Vladimir Katriuk's was born, in 1921, the place of his birth was in the Kingdom of Romania.

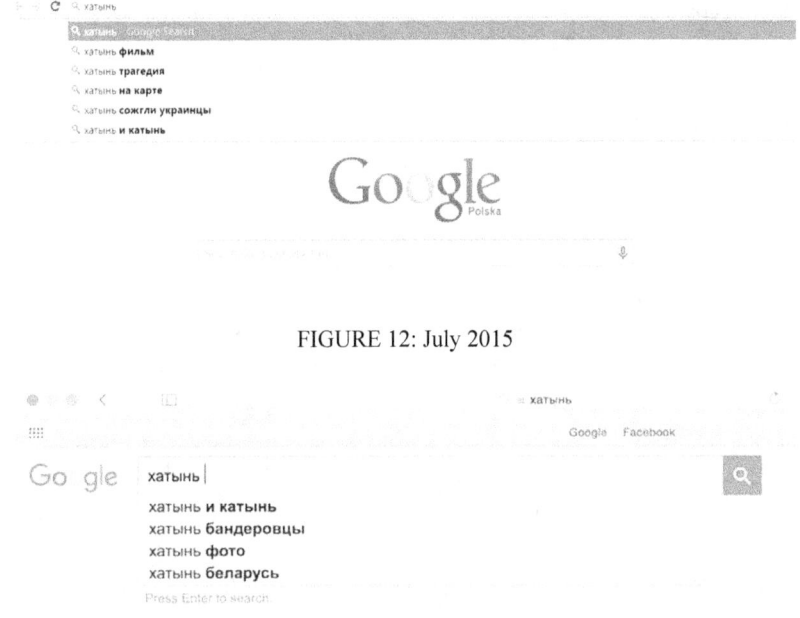

FIGURE 12: July 2015

FIGURE 13: March 2016

Another wave of interest in Vladimir Katriuk emerged on 8 May 2015, when the Russian Federation – as the 'legal successor' of the USSR – requested the extradition of the Canadian citizen to Russia (Svoboda 2015). The Committee of Inquiry of the Russian Federation started a criminal case accusing Katriuk of genocide (Article 357 of the Criminal Code of the Russian Federation) (Vesti 2015). Notably, the Russian media called Vladimir Katriuk a 'murderer', even though legally a court had never found him guilty. On 27 May 2015, the Deputy Prosecutor-General in Russia, Alexander Zvyagintsev, stated that Canada had refused to extradite Katriuk (Subbotin 2015). On 29 May 2015, the Toronto *Globe and Mail* reported that Vladimir Katriuk had died in hospital on 22 May 2015 at the age of 93 (Tu Thanh Ha 2015).

On the very same day, the Russian newspaper *Vzglyad* published an article questioning whether Vladimir Katriuk had actually died, and compared his case to that of Ivan Demjanjuk[11], who had also been ill during the last months of his trial for the murder of thousands of Jews in the Sobibor concentration camp (Baltacheva and Neroznikova 2015). Another Russian newspaper, *MK - Moskovskiy Komsomolets*, published an article about Katriuk's death citing 'trial materials' against Katriuk from 1999 (Rinaeva, 2015). Remarkably, the link to the materials turned out to be the live

---

[11] For more about the case of John Demjanjuk see L. Douglas, *The Right Wrong Man: John Demjanjuk and the Last Great Nazi War Crimes Trial*, Princeton University Press 2016, 352 p.

journal[12] account of a certain Andrei Svetlako from 2009 (Svetlako 2009). Svetlako claims to have translated the trial documents from English and provided links to the originals. However, at the time of writing, the original links showed no such documents, although original documents on the case can indeed be accessed on the Internet (for example, Canada (Minister of Citizenship and Immigration) v. Katriuk 1999).

Not only does the Belarusian Internet mass-media work closely with the Russian mass-media (because of their common language and media discourse), they are also prone to use similar language when describing Katriuk's death and life. For example, the main Belarusian state newspaper, *Belarus Segodnia – Sovetskaya Belorussiya*, devoted a series of articles to Chatyń during May – June 2015. Certainly, it is possible to link this interest to the upcoming 70th anniversary of the end of the Great Patriotic War[13], which was celebrated on 9 May 2015 and is one of the main contemporary state holidays in Belarus, along with another important date for state propaganda: 22 June (the anniversary of the beginning of the Great Patriotic War – the German invasion of the USSR). However, the fact that articles also appeared in the Russian media cannot be ignored. It is possible that the actions of the Russian Committee of Inquiry forced the Belarusian mass-media to pay additional attention to the story of the Chatyń massacre.

On 6 May 2015, an affiliated newspaper of *Belarus Segodnia – Sovetskaia Belorussiia, Narodnaja Hazieta (People's Newspaper)*, published an interview with the historian Viačaslaŭ Seliameniaŭ, Head of the National Archives of Belarus, who had studied and published on Chatyń (Moskalenko 2015). Seliameniaŭ mentioned Katriuk in his interview and expressed his dismay that the man was still free (Moskalenko 2015).

On 10 May 2015, *Belarus Segodnia – Sovetskaia Belorussiia* published an article about the Russian Committee of Inquiry's request to extradite Vladimir Katriuk (Nosov 2015). Another article on the same topic appeared in the newspaper on 29 May 2015. The article, by one Roman Rud', condemned Canada for refusing to extradite Katriuk to Russia and used highly propagandistic language to describe the 'cynicism' of the Canadian judicial system, also mentioning Katriuk's name in connection with the Ukrainian Insurgent Army (UIA) (Rud' 2015b), although Katriuk had never been part of the UIA. The article was followed by a postscript stating that Vladimir Katriuk had died after the article was initially published in the paper version of the newspaper.

---

[12] Live journal is a free personal blog open to the public.

[13] Note that public spaces in today's Belarus use the Soviet name for the war, the 'Great Patriotic War', which encompasses the period of 1941 – 45. Belarusian scholars use both designations: 'World War II' when they refer to the period 1939 – 45 or about the military operations of the allied forces outside of the Soviet Union, and the 'Great Patriotic War' when they refer to Germany's attack on the Soviet Union as the starting point, including the period of the Nazi occupation of Belarus (A. Katljarchuk, 'World War II Memory Politics: Jewish, Polish and Roma Minorities of Belarus', *The Journal of Belarusian Studies* 2013:1, p. 9 – 10).

The same author published another item about Katriuk the next day, on 30 May 2015. The article conveyed exactly the same information as the story in *Vzglyad* mentioned above, questioning whether Katriuk had in fact died (Rud' 2015a). Rud' used very negative language in his story, claiming that he did not want Katriuk to rest in peace.[14] The author also mentioned that in the 1990s, Katriuk had become an honourable citizen of Chernivtsi, thus demonstrating the connection between the Canadian government and contemporary Ukraine. According to Per Anders Rudling, Katriuk's honourable citizenship of Chernivtsi was only true according to some sources (Rudling 2012, p. 42).

On 5 June 2015, *Narodnaja Hazieta* published a letter from a reader named Valerii Lomako entitled 'Irregular Bees' (Lomako 2015). In the letter, the author called Western democracy 'a strange woman', characterizing it as 'biased, evil and with a bad memory' (Lomako 2015). Lomako also accused foreign countries of trying 'to open our eyes to see their version of the truth about the war' (Lomako 2015), thus conflating Katriuk's case and the issue of his extradition with a constructed negative image of democracy overall, one of the most notorious forms of anti-Western propaganda.

On 12 June 2015, the second largest state-owned newspaper, *Respublika* published a feature by Dmitrii Zhukov and Ivan Kovtun on the Chatyń tragedy. In the article, the authors discussed in detail the history of *Schutzmannschaft Bataillon 118*, the Soviet-era trials against members of the squad, and the life of Katriuk (Zhukov and Kovtun 2015). The data cited in the article were similar to those quoted in the above-mentioned Russian web-sites, focusing on Canada's refusal to extradite Vladimir Katriuk. It also claimed that this decision was linked with the West's deteriorating relations with Russia due to the conflict in Ukraine.[15] Remarkably, journalists used the word 'chekisty,'[16] which continued to carry a derogative connotation long after the collapse of the USSR. However, in this case the authors were stressing the professionalism and hard work of the 'chekisty' in their investigation of Nazi war criminals and portrayed them in a positive light (Zhukov and Kovtun 2015). At the end of the article, the authors mentioned the active participation of Katriuk in the activities of the Ukrainian Orthodox Church in Canada and the fact that he had been designated an honourable citizen of Chernivtsi.

On 19 June 2015, another affiliated newspaper of *Belarus Segodnia-Sovetskaia Belorussiia, Selskaia Gazeta Belorusskaia Niva* published an article by Yuliia

---

[14] A translation of the Russian idiom *pokoitsia z mirom/ mir chyemu-libo prakhu.*

[15] NB: This was related to the strong Ukrainian lobby present in Canada on the official level in state institutions.

[16] Whether these were NKVD or KGB employees depends on the year, as the name of the body changed several times during the Soviet era. They were initially called *chekisty*, from the abbreviation for the Emergency Committee in Russian (*ChK*), the first iteration of the Soviet security police. This term became a common nickname and is still used officially in Belarus.

Bolshakova entitled '"Freedom" of Speech for the sake of Nazism is a Crime' (in Russian – "Svobodnoie" slovo v polzu natsizma prestupno') (Bolshakova 2015). This was the most aggressive article to date published on Katriuk by the *Belarus Segodnia – Sovetskaia Belorussiia* group of newspapers. The author raised the issue of the death of Katriuk and the 'problems' of the global community. Bolshakova called Katriuk 'a threefold scum' and came to the conclusion that 'a society which ignores Nazism can only expect problems like terrorism' (Bolshakova 2015). The author concluded the article with some 'facts' about the threat Belarus is facing from 'weapons, ammunition and drugs' from Ukraine, and the build-up of NATO forces 'on the border with the EU' (Bolshakova 2015).

Another article about Katriuk's death in the state newspaper *Zviazda* was translated from the Russian news site *newsru.com*. It adopted a neutral stance, despite mentioning his Ukrainian nationality in the title of the article (Zviazda 2015), which other neutral publications avoided. Three more articles about the death of Vladimir Katriuk in *Komsomolskaia Pravda v Belarusi* (Savicheva 2015), *kyky.org* (Kyky.org 2015), and *Savvy.by* (Savvy.by 2015) were short, neutral, and only stated that he had died and that the Russian Committee of Inquiry had initiated a criminal case against him (Savvy.by 2015) All three sources used the word 'accused' in the titles of their articles, in contrast to articles by pro-governmental sources which called Katriuk 'a butcher' or 'a murderer.'

On 23 June 2016, yet another state-run regional newspaper, *Naš Čas – Volkovysskaia rayonnaia gazeta*, published an article about Vladimir Katriuk. Nadezhda Zinina, the author, wrote about Russia's extradition request and Canada's refusal to comply (Zinina 2015). Zinina also briefly summarized the history of the *Schutzmannschaft Bataillon* 118, accusing the Canadian government of responding improperly to the genocide of the Slavs and accusing other Western 'democracies' (quotation marks are Zinina's) of having a similar attitude (Zinina 2015). Even though the article was published quite recently, it was not accessible on the newspaper's webpage, only on the webpage's cache. The fact of its unexplained removal is evidence of how easy it is for state mass-media in Belarus to change the content of their websites in order to propagate state-sanctioned views.

All of the main democratically leaning mass-media outlets: *Naša Niva* (Naša Niva 2015), *Charter97* (Charter 97 2015), *Radyjo Racyja* (Radyjo Racyja 2015), *European Radio for Belarus* (European Radio for Belarus 2015), and the Belarusian Service of the *Polish Radio for Abroad* (Polskie Radio dla Zagranicy 2015) published short articles about the death of Vladimir Katriuk in May 28 – 29, 2015. Every article stated that Katriuk was only accused of these crimes and that Russia had requested his extradition. This choice of words contrasted to Belarusian state and Russian media's rhetoric, which presented Katriuk as a murderer. However,

*European Radio for Belarus* did mention his Ukrainian origin and also provided a link to the *Declassified History: Chatyń's Butchers* documentary discussed above.

Compared with the case of Andrei Sawoniuk, the case of Vladimir Katriuk has garnered much more attention in both the Belarusian and Russian mass-media. However, whereas the rhetoric of the media groupings labelled 'neutral' or oppositional did not vary greatly until his death, pro-state media tended to get progressively more negative and sometimes openly aggressive towards their subject. Even the death of Katriuk did not soften their language. The story of Katriuk was also gaining increased circulation since the beginning of the Russian-Ukrainian conflict in 2013 and reached its culmination when the man died in May 2015, two weeks after Russia filed an extradition request.

## Conclusion

Comparing Internet mass-media discourse surrounding two war criminals, Anthony (Andrei) Sawoniuk and Vladimir Katriuk, reveals several main trends. Obviously, the Belarusian Internet media space did not devote as much attention to the first case as it did to the second. However, both stories remained incomplete. The following reasons can explain the differences in the coverage of the two cases.

Firstly, in order to properly investigate Nazi war crimes on Belarusian territory, the involvement of the Belarusian authorities is absolutely necessary. Scholars and members of the general public seeking facts find it difficult to access potentially helpful archives due to the inaccessible and non-transparent nature of the Belarusian KGB. The Belarusian state is very tight-lipped when it comes to both foreign and local researchers, especially with regards to sensitive issues. For this reason, many Nazi war criminals were discovered only after the end of the Cold War when the necessary files were made available to Western states. Generally speaking, this lack of accessible information during the Cold War period often critically delayed prosecutions of World War II war criminals in different parts of the world.[17]

Secondly, the Soviet regime was reluctant to highlight the divisions between various national and ethnic groups in the Soviet Union after World War II. The Soviet government were especially unlikely to admit that Jews had faced a much greater threat during the war than the Soviet population in general. As the official Belarusian discourse on World War II borrows heavily from the Soviet approach to the issue, the Holocaust remains of secondary importance compared with

---

[17] See S. Wilson, "War Criminals in the Post-war World: the Case of Kato Tetsutaro," p. 109, *War in History*, 2015. Vol. 22 (1), pp. 87 – 110; L. Douglas, *The Right Wrong Man: John Demjanjuk and the Last Great Nazi War Crimes Trial*, Princeton University Press, 2016, 352 p.; K. von Lingen, *Holmsselring's Last Battle: War Crimes Trials and Cold War Politics 1945 - 1960*, Lawrence, KS: University Press of Kansas, 2009, 457 p.

discussion of the losses of the Belarusian people during the war. Therefore, the crimes of Anthony Sawoniuk, which were committed mainly against Jews, lacked relevance for the official discourse. In contrast, information about Vladimir Katriuk and his involvement in the Chatyń massacre provoked a much greater reaction in the Belarusian media, and various publications began actively disseminating information. The importance of the Chatyń massacre as a symbol for the tragedy of the Belarusian people in World War II in contemporary state ideology was a determining factor for media coverage of Valdimir Katriuk, who was allegedly part of the battalion responsible for the massacre. Meanwhile, the participation of Katriuk's battalion in *aktions* against the Jews was neglected due to the fact that Belarusian suffering overshadowed the Holocaust in Belarusian official discourse.

Thirdly, the year 1999, when the trial against Sawoniuk took place, was a very important time in the contemporary history of Belarus. In that year several political opponents of the Belarusian President disappeared and have not been found since; many people were demanding fair presidential elections and Belarus had entered the Union State of Belarus and Russia, which people feared might lead to the loss of the country's independence. These events became crucial for the further consolidation of the Belarusian regime, and neither the authorities nor the general population could be bothered by a trial taking place in the United Kingdom to investigate the murders of the Jewish population of a small town in Brest region during World War II. The internal and external political situation also played a huge role in the emergence of discussion of Vladimir Katriuk's crimes in 2013–2015. Discussions of war criminals would become important to the Belarusian public only under certain political circumstances.

Moreover, technological progress and the rapid proliferation of the world wide web led to better coverage of the Katriuk case, which occurred in an environment of greater internet connectivity. The fact that both the number of Internet users and on-line sources have substantially increased since 1999 also partially explains why much more information was released about Vladimir Katriuk than Anthony Sawoniuk.

In conclusion, the apathy of contemporary Belarusian authorities towards alternative narratives of the 'glorious' Great Patriotic War, the intensive indoctrination of the Soviet era, and the lack of opportunities to raise awareness of the Holocaust in the present political context make bringing the Holocaust to the fore of Belarusian public discourse highly unlikely. Even though information is becoming more widely available, the chances of Nazi war criminals being discovered (many of whom are now dead of natural causes) remain minimal at present. However, it is indisputable that researchers investigating the crimes of those who participated in the execution of the Belarusian population also had to deal with the Holocaust; they played a valuable role in identifying such criminals while seeking justice for those responsible for one of the cruellest genocides in human history.

In analysing materials on the Belarusian Internet about Sawoniuk and Katriuk several trends emerged. First of all, it is clear that the Russian and Belarusian information spaces overlap greatly, especially with regards to state-owned publications. Not only the sources and information, but also the language and semantics used by Belarusian pro-government journalists are very similar to those utilized by their Russian counterparts.

Secondly, as a result of this above-mentioned overlap, Russian propaganda has a profound influence on the Belarusian mass-media and Belarusian propaganda. Very often the texts of Belarusian official mass-media closely echo their Russian analogues. Moreover, even Russian external and internal politics provoke certain topics in the Belarusian state-owned media. This is not the case for 'neutral' or opposition newspapers, which usually try to remain objective or even oppose the messages of Russian mass-media.

Thirdly, the heroes and 'butchers' of the Great Patriotic War will remain a hot topic in Belarusian mass-media as long as the Great Patriotic War remains a central component of the contemporary propaganda of the Belarusian state. As such an approach is also gradually becoming more popular in Russia, Belarus's main strategic partner, the Great Patriotic War will undoubtedly continue to be treated as 'glorious' in the foreseeable future, depending on how long the Belarusian and Russian presidents remain in power.

## Bibliography

### *Published sources*

Baltacheva, M., Neroznikova, Ye., 2015. Soobschenie o smerti 'khatynskogo palacha' vyglyadit somnitelnym, *Vzgliad.* Available at: <http://www.vz.ru/politics/2015/5/29/747997.html>. [Accessed 06 July 2015].

BBC (1999a). *UK. Sawoniuk – a hidden life exposed.* 1 April 1999. Available at: <http://news.bbc.co.uk/2/hi/uk_news/309937.stm >. [Accessed on 7 April 2015].

BBC (1999b). *UK. Sawoniuk jail term dispute.* 24 June 1999. Available at: < http://news.bbc.co.uk/2/hi/uk_news/376803.stm >. [Accessed on 7 April 2015].

Belaruspartisan, 2012. *U Kanadzie adšukany padazravajemy u datyčanašci da spaĺvannia Chatyni.* Available at: <http://www.belaruspartisan.org/bel/life/210099/>. [Accessed 02 February 2015].

Bolshakova, Yu., 2015. 'Svobodnoie' slovo v polzu natsizma prestupno, *Belorusskaia Niva.* Available at: <http://belniva.sb.by/obshchestvo-4/article/svobodnoe-slovo-v-polzu-natsizma-prestupno.html>. [Accessed 06 July 2015].

Charter 97, 2015. *Abvinavačany u zabojstvach žycharoú Chatyni pamior u Kanadzie.* Available at: < http://charter97.org/be/news/2015/5/29/153407/>. [Accessed 05 July 2015].

Chatyń Memorial Complex, 2005. *Trahiedyja Chatyni.* Available at: <http://www.khatyn.by/by/tragedy/>. [Accessed 01 February 2015].

Dalidovič, J., and Marozava, S., 2013. Kryvavy slied Chatynskich kataŭ, *Zviazda, 18 October 2013.* Available at: <http://zviazda.by/2013/10/19149.html>. [Accessed 02 February 2015].

Datsyk, V.V., 2006. A. Savoniuk, *Domachevo.com.* Available at: <http://domachevo.com/historu-news-ru.htm>. [Accessed 02 February 2015].

Dykhovichnaia, O., and Moloslavov, A., 2008. *Pozornaia taina Khatyni,* Super Reality. *Youtube.com.* Available at: <https://www.youtube.com/watch?v=px6r9XgT2q0>. [Accessed 05 April 2016].

European Radio for Belarus, 2015. *U Kanadzie pamior abvinavačany pa spravie spaliennia bielaruskaj vioski Chatyń.* Available at: <http://euroradio.fm/u-kanadze-pamyor-abvinavachany-pa-sprave-spalennya-belaruskay-vyoski-hatyn>. [Accessed 06 July 2015].

European Radio for Belarus, 2012. *U Kanadzie znajšli adnaho z 'chatynskich kataŭ'.* Available at: <http://euroradio.fm/report/u-kanadze-znaishli-adnago-z-khatynskikh-kataw-106113 >. [Accessed 01 February 2015].

Holubieŭ, V., 1999. Vneshniaia politika respubliki Belarus. Fevral' 1999 goda, *Hrights.ru.* Available at: <http://www.hrights.ru/text/belorus/b11/Chapter3.htm>. [Accessed 02 February 2015].

Kalinoŭski, V. 1999. Old Bailey sudzić Antona Savaniuka, *Naša Niva, 04 (125).* Available at: <http://nn.by/?c=ar&i=93302>. [Accessed 02 February 2015].

Kirkievič, A., 2014. Chatyń: chto spaliŭ bielaruskuju viosku, *Novy čas,* 16 February 2014. Available at: <http://novychas.info/poviaz_casou/chatynj_zorstkaje_recha_histor/>. [Accessed 02 February 2015].

Kobiak, R., 1999. Bez sroka davnosti, *Vechernii Minsk,* 16 February 1999. Available at: <http://www.vminsk.by/news/30/11923/>. [Accessed 02 February 2015].

Kovtun, I., and Zhukov, D., 2015. Krovavye dela khatynskikh palachei, *Respublika,* 12 June 2015. Available at: <http://respublika.sb.by/obshchestvo-27/article/krovavye-dela-khatynskikh-palachey.html>. [Accessed 06 July 2015].

Krapivin, S., 2005. Otdal dushu dyavolu Anton Savoniuk, *Sovetskaia Belorussiia, 9 November 2005.* Available at: <http://tv.sb.by/obshchestvo/article/otdal-dushu-dyavolu-anton-savonyuk.html>. [Accessed 01 February 2015].

Kuzovenkov, M., 2014. Rassekrechennaia istoriia. Palachi Khatyni. Bez sroka davnosti, *Tvkultura.ru, Telekompaniia 'Pod zankom Pi'.* Available at: <https://www.youtube.com/watch?t=32&v=B1TOVqukYQc>. [Accessed 06 July 2015].

Kyky.org, 2015. *Obviniaemyi v ubiistvakh zhitelei Khatyni Vladimir Katriuk umer v Kanade,* 29 May 2015. Available at: <http://kyky.org/news/obvinyaemyy-v-ubiystvah-zhiteley-hatyni-vladimir-katryuk-umer-v-kanade>. [Accessed 06 July 2015].

Lashkevich, K., 2010. Poslednii 'belorusskii' natsist dozhivaet v Estonii?, *Tut.by,* 26 August 2010. Available at: <http://news.tut.by/society/195137.html>. [Accessed 02 February 2015].

Lomako, V., 2015. Nepravilnye pchely, *Narodnaja Hazieta,* 05 May 2015. Available at: <http://ng.sb.by/stati/article/nepravilnye-pchely43.html>. [Accessed 06 July 2015].

Maksimov, S. S., 1979. Istoriia odnogo predatelstva, *Neotvratimoie vozmezdiie: Po materialam sudebnykh protsessov nad izmennikami Rodiny, fashistkimi palachami i agentami imperialisticheskich razvedok,* Moskva, 294 p. *Voiennaia literatura.* Available at: <http://militera.lib.ru/h/sb_neotvratimoe_vozmezdie/12.html>. [Accessed 06 March 2016].

Moskalenko, G., 2015. Tragediia 'vohniennych viosak', *Narodnaja Hazieta,* 06 May 2015. Available at: <http://ng.sb.by/stati/article/tragediya-vognennykh-vyesak.html>. [Accessed 06 July 2015].

Naviny, 2012. *V Kanade nashli odnogo iz palachei Khatyni?* Available at: <http://naviny.by/rubrics/society/2012/04/27/ic_articles_116_177672/>. [Accessed 01 February 2015].

Naša Niva, 2012. *U Kanadzie adšukany padazravany u datyčanaści da spalvannia Chatyni.* Available at: <http://nn.by/?c=ar&i=72602>. [Accessed 02 February 2015].

Naša Niva, 2015. *U Kanadzie pamior 93-hadovy Uladzimir Katruk, abvinavačany pa spravie spaliennia Chatyni.* Available at: < http://nn.by/?c=ar&i=150383 >. [Accessed 05 July 2015].

Nosov, Ye., 2015. SK RF vozbudil ugolovnoie delo v otnoshenii 93-letnego uchatnika ubiistv v Khatyni, *Sovetskaia Belorussiia,* 10 May 2015. Available at: <http://www.sb.by/v-belarusi/article/sk-rf-vozbudil-ugolovnoe-dela-v-otnoshenii-93-letnego-uchastnika-ubiystv-v-khatyni.html>. [Accessed 06 July 2015].

NTV, 2012. *Prestarelyi pchelovod okazalsia massovym ubiitsei.* Available at: <http://www.ntv.ru/novosti/293479/>. [Accessed 02 February 2015].

Polskie Radio dla Zagranicy, 2015. *U Kanadzie pamior abvinavačany ŭ datyčanaści da zabojstvaŭ u Chatyni.* Available at: < http://tinyurl.com/hx3txqg >. [Accessed 06 July 2015].

Pruitt, S., 2015. *10 most wanted Nazi War criminals.* <http://www.history.com/news/history-lists/10-most-wanted-nazis?cmpid=Social_FBPAGE_HISTORY_20151108_271697851&linkId=18600176>. [Accessed on 20 November 2016].

Radyjo Racyja, 2015. *U Kanadzie pamior abvinavačany ŭ zabojstvach žycharoŭ Chatyni.* Available at: <http://www.racyja.com/hramadstva/u-kanadze-pamyor-abvinavachany-u-zabojs/>. [Accessed 05 July 2015].

Rassekrechennaia istoriia, 2014. *Tvkultura.ru, Telekompaniia 'Pod zankom Pi'.* Available at: <http://tvkultura.ru/video/show/brand_id/31793/episode_id/993367/>. [Accessed 06 July 2015].

Respublika, 2012. *Ulei dla palacha Khatyni.* Available at: <http://tinyurl.com/jcsdene >. [Accessed 02 February 2015].

Rinaeva, I., 2015. Pochemu karatel' Khatyni Katriuk schastlivo prozhil v Kanade do 93 let, *MK,* 29 May 2015. Available at: <http://www.mk.ru/social/2015/05/29/karatel-khatyni-katryuk-skonchalsya-v-kanade-beznakazannym.html>. [Accessed 06 July 2015].

Rud', R., 2015a. Ne pozhelaiu mira ego prakhu, *Sovetskaia Belorussiia,* 101, 30 May 2015. Available at: <http://www.sb.by/obshchestvo/article/ne-pozhelayu-mira-ego-prakhu.html>. [Accessed 06 July 2015].

Rud', R., 2015b. On zheg Khatyn, a seichas blagodenstvuiet v Kanade, *Sovetskaia Belorussiia,* 100, 29 May 2015. Available at: <http://www.sb.by/obshchestvo/article/on-zheg-khatyn-a-seychas-blagodenstvuet-v-kanade.html>. [Accessed 06 July 2015].

Savicheva, A., 2015. V Kanade skonchalsia Vladimir Katriuk, obvinyaemyi v ubiistvakh v Khatyni, *Komsomolskaia Pravda v Belarusi.* Available at: <http://www.kp.by/online/news/2069099>. [Accessed 06 July 2015].

Savvy.by, 2015. *V vozraste 93 let skonchalsia obvinyaemyi v khatynskikh ubiistvakh Vladimir Katriuk.* Available at: <http://www.savvy.by/novosti/politika/evropa/item/2984-chatjn.html>. [Accessed 06 July 2015].

Sil'nye novosti, 2012. *V Kanade obnaruzhili ukrainskogo politsaia prichastnogo k sozhzheniiu Khatyni.* Available at: <http://odsgomel.org/rus/news/belarus/23377/>. [Accessed 01 February 2015].

Svaboda, 2005. *Viadomy bielaruski palicaj pamior u brytanskaj turmie.* Available at: <http://www.svaboda.org/content/article/802247.html>. [Accessed 01 February 2015].

Svetlako, A., 2009. Vladimir Katriuk – ot palacha do pasechnika, *Livejournal.* Available at: <http://svetlako.livejournal.com/29501.html>. [Accessed 06 July 2015].

Svoboda, 2015. *Umer podozrevayemyi v voiennykh prestupleniiakh Vladimir Katriuk.* Available at: <http://www.svoboda.org/content/article/27042800.html>. [Accessed 06 July 2015].

Subbotin, I., 2015. Kanada otkazalas' vydat' Rossii obvinyaemogo v genotside v Khatyni Katriuka, *MK,* 27 May 2015. Available at: <http://www.mk.ru/social/2015/05/27/kanada-otkazalas-vydat-rossii-obvinyaemogo-v-genocide-v-khatyni-katryuka.html >. [Accessed 06 July 2015].

Supruniuk, A., 1999. Naviny 19 liutaha 1999 hoda, *Svaboda.org.* Available at: <http://www.svaboda.org/content/article/24829574.html>. [Accessed 02 February 2015].

The Guardian, 2005. *Nazi war criminal Sawoniuk dies in jail.* 7 November 2005. Available at: <https://www.theguardian.com/uk/2005/nov/07/secondworldwar.world>. [Accessed 05 October 2016].

Tu Thanh Ha, 2015. Alleged Nazi war criminal died two weeks after Russia sought extradition, *The Globe and Mail.* Available at: <http://www.theglobeandmail.com/news/national/vladimir-katriuk-died-two-weeks-after-russia-sought-extradition/article24707200/ >. [Accessed 06 July 2015].

Udf.by, 2012. *V Kanade naiden podozrevaemyi v prichastnosti k sozhzheniiu v Khatyni.* Available at: <http://udf.by/news/society/58920-v-kanade-nayden-podozrevaemyy-v-prichastnosti-k-sozhzheniyu-hatyni.html>. [Accessed 01 February 2015].

Vesti, 2015. *Ubiitsa zhitelei Khatyni Vladimir Katriuk skonchalsia v Kanade.* Available at: <http://www.vesti.ru/doc.html?id=2615696>. [Accessed 06 July 2015].

Zinina, N., 2015. Vladimir Katriuk – poslednii karatel' Khatyni, *Naš Čas.* Available at: <http://tinyurl.com/jcgbflt>. [Accessed 06 July 2015].

Zviazda, 2015. *U Kanadzie pamior ukrainiec Uladzimir Katruk, jakoha u Rasii sabralisia sudzić za zabojstva žycharoŭ Chatyni.* Available at: <http://zviazda. by/2015/05/85507.html>. [Accessed 06 July 2015].

**Secondary literature**

Applebaum, A., 1999. The Nightmarish World That Awaits a British Jury, *The Sunday Telegraph,* February 14, issue 1966, 35.

Canada (Minister of Citizenship and Immigration) v. Katriuk, 1999. *Will Zuzak web-site.* Available at: <http://www.telusplanet.net/public/mozuz/katriuk/katriuk991130.html#bottom3.2>. [Accessed 05 April 2016].

Dean, M., 2010. Crime and Comprehension, Punishment and Legal Attitudes. German and Local Perpetrators in Domachevo, Belarus, in the Records of Soviet, Polish, German, and British War Crimes Investigations, p. 265–280, *Holocaust and Justice. Representation and Historiography of the Holocaust in Post-War Trials,* ed. David Bankier, Dan Michman. Jerusalem: Yad Vashem; New York: Berghahn Books.

Douglas, L., 2016. *The Right Wrong Man: John Demjanjuk and the Last Great Nazi War Crimes Trial,* Princeton University Press, 352 p.

Encyklapiedyia historyi Bielarusi. U 6 tamach, 1994. Tom 2. Belick – Himn / Redkal.: B. I. Sačanka [i inš.], Minsk: BelEn., 537 p.; il. Karty.

Evreiskaia obschina v Resublike Belarus', 2004. *Istoriia yevreyev Belarusi.* Available at: <http://www.jewishbelarus.org/index.php?pid=23&lang=ru>. [Accessed 01 February 2015].

Gerlach, C., 1999. *Kalkurierte Morde: Die deutsche Wirtschafts- und Vernichtungspolitik in Weißrußland 1941 bis 1944,* Hamburger Edition, 1999, 1234 p.

Katljarchuk, A., 2013. World War II Memory Politics: Jewish, Polish and Roma Minorities of Belarus, *The Journal of Belarusian Studies,* pp. 7–37.

Lingen, K. von, 2009. *Kesselring's Last Battle: War Crimes Trials and Cold War Politics, 1945–1960,* Lawrence, KS: University Press of Kansas, 457 p.

Marples, D. R., 2014. *'Our Glorious Past': Lukashenka's Belarus and the Great Patriotic War,* Stuttgart: Ibidem Verlag, 403 p.

Rudling, P. A., 2013a. The Invisible Genocide: the Holocaust in Belarus, in *Bringing the Dark Past to Light,* eds. J. – P. Himka and J. B. Michlic, University of Nebraska Press, pp. 59–82.

Rudling, P. A., 2012. The Khatyn Massacre in Belorussia: a Historical Controversy Revisited, *Holocaust and Genocide Studies,* 26, no. 1 (Spring), pp. 29–58.

Rudling, P. A., 2011. Terror and Local Collaboration in Occupied Belarus: the Case of the Schutzmannschaft Batallion 118. I. Background, *Historical Yearbook,* vol. VIII, Romanian Academy, "Nicolae Iorga" History Institute, Bucharest, pp. 195–214.

Rudling, P. A., 2013b. Nieprykmietny hienacyd: Chalakost u Bielarusi, *ARCHE,* 2, July, pp. 120–139.

Vsesoiuznaia perepis' naseleniia, 1939. Natsional'nyi sostav naseleniia po respublikam SSSR. *Demoskop Weekly*. Available at: <http://demoscope.ru/weekly/ssp/sng_nac_39.php?reg=3 >. [Accessed 20 April 2016].

Vsesoiuznaia perepis' naseleniia, 1959. Natsional'nyi sostav naseleniya po respublikam SSSR. *Demoskop Weekly.* Available at: <http://demoscope.ru/weekly/ssp/sng_nac_59.php?reg=3 >. [Accessed 20 April 2016].

Wiesenthal Center Annual Report, 2013. *Wiesenthal Center.* Available at: <http://www.wiesenthal.com/atf/cf/%7B54d385e6-f1b9-4e9f-8e94-890c3e6dd277%7D/NAZI-WAR-CRIMINALS-REPORT_2013.PDF>. [Accessed 01 February 2015].

Wiesenthal Center Annual Report, 2014. *Wiesenthal Center.* Available at: <http://www.wiesenthal.com/atf/cf/%7B54d385e6-f1b9-4e9f-8e94-890c3e6dd277%7D/WIESENTHAL-CENTER_2014-ANNUAL-NAZI-WAR-CRIMNAL-REPORT-V.2.PDF >. [Accessed 01 February 2015].

Wilson, S., 2015. War Criminals in the Post-War World: the Case of Kato Tetsutaro, *War in History*, Vol. 22 (1), pp. 87–110.

# Belarus: from a Social Contract to a Security Contract?

## 2016 Annual London Lecture on Belarusian Studies

BY

ANDREW WILSON

In 2014 Aliaksandr Lukashenka reached his twentieth anniversary as President of Belarus, prompting a series of analyses of just how he had managed to survive in power for so long. The best of these need only refinement. Margarita Balmaceda, for example looks, at how Lukashenka has both extracted rent from Russia by exploiting his foreign policy value and used it skilfully to consolidate his hold on power. Russian subsidies maintain the Belarusian economy; but, she writes, 'while financial support from Russia has been key (in which access to external energy rents played an important role), no less important is the way these rents were used domestically' (Balmaceda 2014a, 515). Other studies by Pranevičiūtė-Neliupšienė and Maksimiuk (2014, 124-156), Ioffe (2014; Ioffe and Yarashevich 2011) and Yarashevich (2014) of what might be called 'distributional authoritarianism' have looked at the regime's spending on social goods to maintain baseline popularity and keep the level of coercion lower than it would be otherwise.

Ironically, however, this analysis came at the very time when the old paradigm was changing. The war in Ukraine, Russia's increasingly problematic relations with all of its neighbours and Russia's own economic troubles put both the subsidy regime and Lukashenka's foreign policy balancing game in doubt. Lukashenka won official re-election in 2015; but this was the first time he had held an election in a recession, with the supply of social goods under threat. The maintenance of statehood and national security have suddenly become a much more prominent part of his governing formula, but it remains to be seen how secure that will make his rule in the future.

In other words, just when we had some pretty good answers to explain how Belarus works and how Lukashenka has survived for so long, we need to know more.

## Economic Risks

Belarus has had three recessions since 2008. The first was in the global recession year of 2009. The second came after an unsustainable spending surge to get Lukashenka through the 2010 election. Official statistics still showed growth in 2011, but the Belarusian rouble lost 60% of its value and inflations topped 108% in a crisis atmosphere, until a Russian bail-out was agreed in November 2011. This briefly restored the system whereby Russian subsidies provided 15-16% of Belarusian GDP (Aliachnovič 2015). But once Russia was hit by economic sanctions after its aggression against Ukraine in 2014, it could no longer afford to be so generous. With relations with the IMF on ice since 2010, only $800 million came in 2016 from the Russia-led Eurasian Fund.

Belarus also lost exports to Russia and Ukraine as both countries suffered GDP loss, only partly compensated by some import switching and re-routing and re-labelling of goods under EU sanction against Russia. An anaemic recovery in Belarus in 2012-13 was therefore followed by a much-deeper recession beginning in 2014, compounded by the fall in the oil price.

But Lukashenka rejected root-and-branch reform in his fifth inauguration speech in November 2015: arguing that «This would mean smashing the political system, the entire government of Belarus, in pieces, dividing and giving away the state and people's property" (Deutsche Welle 2015). Nevertheless, money-saving reforms have been inevitable; state employment and pensions were gradually trimmed through 2014-16.

FIGURE 1: Belarusian GDP Growth, 2009-2017 (source: World Bank, IMF)

| 2009 | 0.2 |
|------|-----|
| 2010 | 7.7 |
| 2011 | 5.5 |
| 2012 | 1.7 |
| 2013 | 1.1 |
| 2014 | 1.7 |
| 2015 | -3.9 |
| 2016 | -2.7 |
| 2017 | 0.4 |

## Security Risks

Belarus has also had to reassess its security situation since 2014. Despite Minsk being a traditional ally of Moscow, all of Russia's neighbours, friend or foe, were shaken by the assault on Ukrainian sovereignty beginning in 2014. And Russia clearly has an option on 'Operation Belarus'. Russian nationalists have been given license to criticise Lukashenka for his lack of loyalty, and his shift towards, or firmer embrace of, some kind of statist nationalism, since 2014. Networks like zapadrus.su and imperiya. by are promoting the old nineteenth century idea of Belarus as 'West Russia', and have attacked 'Litvinism' – depicting the idea of an independent and Western Belarus as an artificial emanation of the 'foreign' Grand Duchy of Litva (normally mislabelled in English as the Grand Duchy of Lithuania) (Popov 2016). Periodic trade wars, despite Belarus being a member of the Eurasian Economic Union, have ratcheted up the tension. The row over the military base at Babruisk rumbles on. Belarus does not yet face the threat of 'hybrid war', but according to one commentator 'there has lately been an outburst of activity from various previously dormant [pro-Russian] organisations in Belarus. These include Cossack organisations, unions of Afghan war veterans, Orthodox youth camps, patriotic military clubs, and others' (Karatch 2016a).

Belarus does not have any obvious pro-Russian redoubt, like Crimea or the Donbas. It does not have any equivalent of the Yanukovych 'Family' making trouble. But the Orthodox Church is seen as too pro-Russian (Lukashenka was angry that he was not even consulted when an ethnic Russian was appointed to head the Church in 2013), and has been linked to the growing number of 'Cossack' and veterans' groups.

Underlying all this is the broader problem that the old foreign policy paradigm has broken down. Belarus had a 'balanced' foreign policy, but its primary relationship was with Russia, where as Balmaceda put it, Belarus had two main strategies to extract resources: playing up to Russia's collective self-esteem and selling the idea of the 'ally of last resort'. Both strategies were predicated on there being only *one* axis of hostility, between Russia and the West. Then, according to Balmaceda, 'a certain regularity could be observed: every time relations between Russia and the West worsened, the relative value of Belarus as an ally increased' (Balmaceda 2014b, 120).

But now there are two lines of tension – between Russia and the West and between Russia and its neighbours. So the old foreign policy position of maximum advantage for Belarus – that Belarus is a pro-Russian power with autonomy to act in its own interests – is now seen in Moscow as the position of an insufficiently enthusiastic ally and a potential defector. And Belarus cannot simply return to the position of 'ally of last resort' because it has to think about its own national security first.

Lukashenka changed the military doctrine in 2015 to guard against any appearance of 'little green men' in Belarus. As it now reads, the 'sending of armed groups, irregular armed forces, mercenary groups, or regular armed forces who use arms against the Republic of Belarus by a foreign country or countries or on behalf of a foreign country or countries' will trigger a declaration of war (Coalson and Jozwiak, 2015). In 2016 a revised version talked of the dual threat of 'hybrid warfare' and 'colour revolutions', but with the implication that Russia could exploit the latter.

Defence spending is edging up, from 1.6% of GDP in 2012 to 1.97% in 2014 ($710 million in total, though $640 million net). There are 59,500 service personnel, including 46,000 soldiers and 13,000 civilians. Plans to build a 120,000-strong territorial defence force out of 350,000 reservists may prove a pipe-dream, however, like most 'people's militias'.

But Belarus is at least quantitatively and qualitatively better off than Ukraine in early 2014, despite having less than a quarter of the population. The recent release of the transcript of the Ukrainian National Security and Defence Council meeting the day after Russia began the annexation of Crimea (28 February 2014) showed just how easy it had been for the Russians to take over the peninsula. The new Minister of Defence Ihor Tenyukh spells out the situation: 'I'll speak frankly. Today we have no army. It was systematically destroyed by Yanukovych and his entourage (Rettman 2016).' Ukraine could mobilise only 5,000 troops and needed these to defend Kyiv.

## Is Lukashenka Out-of-step with Public Opinion?

For reasons of personal survival and raison d'état, Lukashenka has asserted his relative independence since 2014. He has claimed that 'Belarus is not part of the Russian world' (Novaia gazeta 2015). He has promised that 'every Belarusian can rest assured that no one will ever be allowed to destabilize the situation in the country, violate its sovereignty and integrity' (Website of the President of Belarus 2016) and 'Belarus will not allow itself to be drawn into any political adventures' (Minsk-Novosti 2016). His 2010 election slogan 'For a Strong and Prosperous Belarus' was changed in 2015 to 'For the Future of Independent Belarus!' His 2015 election programme co-opted the nationalist argument that: 'Two decades ago, we started to build a new country - the first independent Belarusian state in history. For centuries, we have walked towards independence. History did not spare us. She did not give us an easy path. Our soil does not possess fabulous wealth - and we have always gained our bread with hard but honest work. They have tried to conquer us from outside and divide us inside.' And he defined his 'first important task' as ensuring that 'BELARUS WILL ALWAYS BE FREE AND INDEPENDENT! (Belarus Segodnia 2015)'.

But public opinion in Belarus has moved in contradictory directions. On the one hand, Belarusians want stability. Ordinary Belarusians tend to see the trope of Ukraine's 'Maidan' as a threat to order rather than a path to liberty; only 10% supported possible public protests before the 2015 election (Shraibman 2015). Only 15% would join in even economic protests (IISEPS 2015a). The fear of unrest is widespread (Bohdan 2015).

According to a June 2015 poll, only 23.2% of Belarusians viewed the fall of Yanukovych positively; 63.2% were negative. A striking 50.9% consider the new

Ukrainian government 'fascist', and 15% do not think that Petro Poroshenko is a legitimate president of Ukraine (Mojeiko 2015a). (Nearly all the opinion polls quoted are by IISEPS, the Independent Institute of Socio-Economic and Political Studies. It has a bad habit of asking leading questions, but was still the best polling organisation in Belarus. It was ordered to be closed in 2016). A majority, 54.7%, of respondents considered Yanukovych's removal a coup-d'état, while only 27.7% thought to be 'a fair retribution for the bloodshed that occurred' (Smok 2014). Only15.5% of Belarusians said they might take part in a hypothetical Belarusian Maidan; 10.7% said they would side with the authorities; while by far the biggest number, 65.3%, would remain neutral (Yeliseyeu 2014).

When asked in June 2015 what they would do 'If Russia tried to annex Belarus' or part of Belarus, only 18.7 per cent said they would 'resist with arms', and only 12.1 per cent would 'welcome the changes'. A massive 52.8 per cent said they would 'try to adapt to the new situation' (IISEPS 2015b).

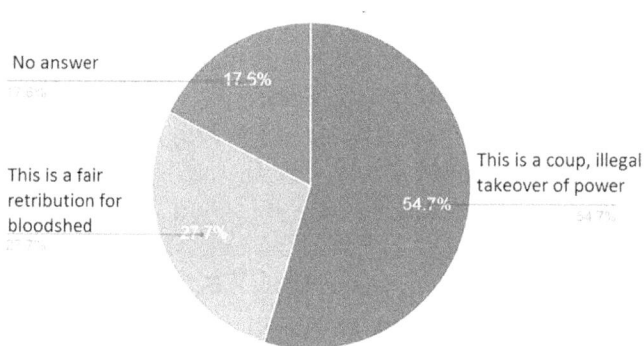

FIGURE 2. President Yanukovych was ousted in Ukraine.
What do you think of these developments? (Source: Smok 2014)

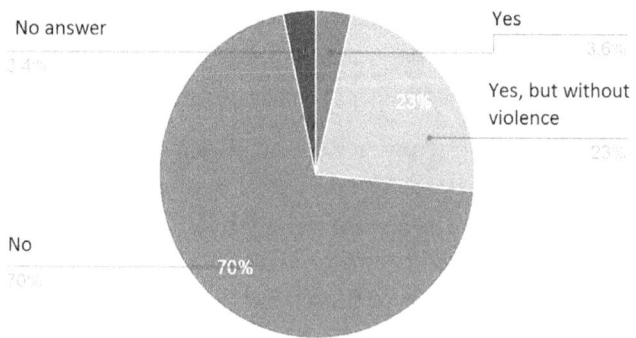

FIGURE 3: Would you like events similar to in Ukraine to happen in Belarus?
(Source: Smok 2014)

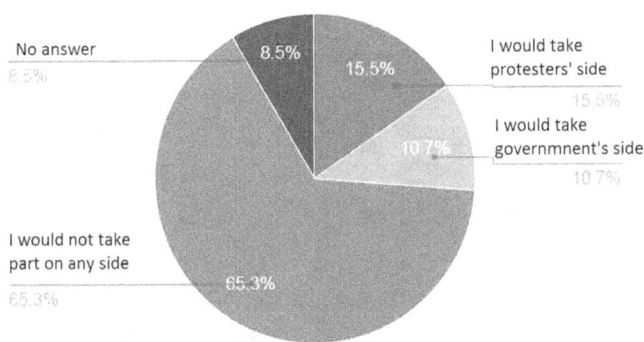

FIGURE 4: If events similar to Ukraine happened in Belarus,
would you take part in them? (Source: Smok 2014)

When asked another strongly leading questions after Russia's annexation of Crimea in the summer of 2014, 26.9% of Belarusians agreed that it was 'imperial seizure, annexation', compared to 62.2% who chose the option that it was 'the return of Russia of Russian lands, the restoration of historical justice'. When asked to assess the situation in Donetsk and Luhansk 65.5% endorsed the chosen wording that 'it is a popular protest against illegitimate power', as against 23.2% who opted for the description of the events as 'rebellion (*miatezh*), organised by Russia' (IISEPS 2014a).

## Sobering up. A little

What would you do if Russia tried to annex all or part of Belarus' territory?

FIGURE 5: Source: A poll by the Independent Institute
of Socio-economic and Political Studies (IISEPS)

The idea of the 'Russian world', which Lukashenka rejected and Putin used to justify the annexation of Crimea, is regarded positively by 32.3% of Belarusians and 15.1% are negative, though again 44.8% are indifferent (IISEPS 2015c).

Support for the EU dropped to 25% in 2014; while in Ukraine, according to Pew, it has gone up to 67% (Simmons 2015). Support for rival integration projects with the West and with Russia had been surprisingly even in Belarus before 2014. In fact, foreign policy preferences in Belarus might best be treated as a dependent variable - a relatively fluid category determined as much by political ebb-and-flow as the other way around (White and Feklyunina 2014).

IISEPS have a longstanding question 'If you had to choose between integration with Russia and joining the European Union, what choice would you make?' Answers have not been set in stone but have tended to follow whatever seemed the most feasible foreign policy option at the time. Looking at the period either side of the 2010 election, support for integration with Russia fell from 35.7% in December 2008 to a low of 29% in December 2011, as relations with Russia deteriorated; rising back a little as relations got back on track, but then falling again after 2014. Support for the EU correspondingly rose to a high of 48.6% in March 2011 – for the first time considerably higher than support for Russia - and then fell back to a low of 25.1% in June 2015 (IISEPS 2015d). A tentative explanation would be that economic concerns crowded out security concerns in 2011, making the EU relatively attractive, but security fears intruded after 2014.

In fact, the number of 'don't knows' may be going up. In a December 2015 IISEPS survey, only 19.8% would vote to join the EU, and 29.7% would support the integration of Belarus and Russia. So the number of neutrals and don't knows was almost half.

This is even clearer when it comes to attitudes towards the war in Ukraine: 77% of Belarusians oppose any involvement on either side (IISEPS 2014b). A new law in 2016 made it an offence for Belarusian citizens to fight on either side (Drakakhrust 2016a). Lukashenka has dragged his feet on the proposed Russian air base (Belarus is home to two Russian '*obyekty*' , a naval communications centre at Viliejka and a radar base at HancaviČy, but no equivalent of the Black Sea base from which Russia launched its coup in Crimea). Interestingly, many Belarusians agree that a base might destabilise more than it protects – in one poll only 27% of respondents backed the base idea, while 33.9% were opposed and 31.2% were indifferent (Drakakhrust 2016b).

But support for the Russian position and the Russian version of events is still strong. Most Belarusians watch Russian TV. According to one analysis, '73.1% of respondents from Belarus responded in December 2014 that they trusted (to a varying degree) the Russian Media' (Karatch 2016b). State-owned ANT is technically the most popular channel, 'but ANT is popular because of the Russian TV shows that it rebroadcasts. The top five most viewed ANT broadcasts include four Russian and one joint Belarusian-Russian show' (Astapenia and Balkunets

2016, 18). On the other hand, the number watching Russia TV has fallen from 90% to 80% in two years (Astapenia and Balkunets 2016, 19). It will be interesting to see if state propaganda on Belarusian TV and other media can shift public opinion in a more 'statist' direction.

## National Identity

Lukashenka's defence of independence was enough to disarm some, if not all, of the traditional opposition. Unlike 2010, there were few calls for protests during the 2015 election, in case Russia used a 'Belarusian Maidan' as an excuse to intervene (tut.by 2015). Though part of the 'new moderate' opposition was accused by the old radical opposition of covert links with, or support from, the presidency (Rutkowski, Rychły and Zaniewicz 2016). Tentative moves to row back on Lukashenka's previous neglect of Belarusian language and culture were also clearly designed to further this rapprochement (Mojeiko 2015b).

It was significant that the two symbolic opposition members 'allowed' to win seats in the 2016 parliamentary elections represented these two wings – the moderate and the cultural opposition. But how far Lukashenka can take this managed rapprochement remains to be seen. Steps towards political technology pluralism have always been likely. But as critic Aliaksandr Klaskoŭski has pointed out, Lukashenka is "afraid of developing national self-consciousness because this will strengthen civil society, which is critical of his regime. It [the regime] talks a lot about patriotism," he continues, "but real as opposed to state-controlled patriots make it uncomfortable'" (Goble 2016).

Belarus does not yet have a strong national identity that would automatically align both society and elites with Lukashenka in his defence of independence. What might be dubbed 'soft' alignment with Russian culture is still stronger than 'soft' alignment with the Western version of the Belarusian idea. Lukashenka has increasingly represented a 'creolic' middle ground, but not one that is capable of transcending this fundamental divide. But it's time to look properly at questions of state –led nation-building. What ideas and tropes are slowly being attached to the otherwise empty slogan of 'For Belarus!'? The strength of Lukashenka's 'imagined community' is about to be sorely tested. And Lukashenka faces a classic Catch-22 problem: any moves he takes to nationalise Belarus would be perceived as hostile by Russia.

## Is Lukashenka Out-of-step with the Elite?

After more than twenty years in power, the West is belatedly developing a better base in 'Lukashenka studies'. We know very little, however, about the Belarusian elite. We do not know how loyal the state apparatus is to Lukashenka. We don't know enough about the sticks and carrots that keep the elite loyal. We don't know enough about the *whys* and *wherefores* of the periodic purging of apparent loyalists – the case against leading businessman Jury Čyž being only the latest (Bohdan and Astapenia 2016).

We don't know enough about the key mechanisms of state control. Recent works by Balmaceda and Lucan Way have identified some key institutions, but we don't know much about their internal workings. The Committee for Government Control (KGK), for example, oversees the bureaucracy and a network of semi-autonomous businesses. The Presidential Business Administration (UDP) and its Property Management Division act as leaseholders for almost the entire economy. The off-budget Presidential Fund is allegedly used to control key income streams from oil and arms sales. Balmaceda estimates its size at \$3 billion to \$10 billion per annum (Balmaceda 2014b, 102). Lukashenka allegedly takes a 'cut' on most business deals (Balmaceda 2014b, 111), which is potentially the thin end of the wedge away from distributional authoritarianism and towards the kind of top-heavy corruption seen in Ukraine under Yanukovych.

But we don't know how much scope there is for 'informal practices' within the elite – for example, who gets the rent from the shady system of semi-independent oil brokers, *davaltsy* or *neftetreideri*, half-in and half-out of the *sistema*.

We don't know enough about the Belarusian *siloviki* and their ultimate loyalties (Liakhovich 2012). Clearly they are not totally hollowed out and penetrated by agents, as the army and SBU were in Ukraine under Yanukovych. But many are ethnic Russians. And many more served or trained in Russia (many officers and special forces are graduates of the Ryazan Higher airborne Command School and the Special Intelligence faculty of the Novosibirsk school) (Tynchenko 2015). How much do joint exercises and socialisation matter? Aliaksandr Aliesin published an article in March 2015, entitled 'Belarusian army to be retrained for hybrid warfare' – which you can read either way. It's a statement of intent, but also an admission of just how far it was previously integrated with its Russian equivalent.

It would be good to know more about Viktar Lukashenka's powers over the *siloviki*, and how exactly the three branches of KGB, Operational and Analytical Center and the Investigative Committee relate to one another.

Finally, and possibly most importantly, we don't know enough about the non-material loyalty of the elite. Lucan Way has identified a long-term weakness for Lukashenka in the lack of dominant party to bind the elite together and represent its interests (Way 2015). The sheer lack of meaningful public politics in Belarus obviously matters for mass opinion, but it's also a problem for elites. The weakness of Belarusian nationalism, even after twenty two years of Lukashenka, is clearly also a problem.

A study by Matsuzato in 2004 showed how Lukashenka's 'rotation of cadres' seems to be an effective way of preventing the formation of bureaucratic cliques in the regions (Matsuzato 2004).[1] The downside of this policy might be that rotating cadres fail to put down deep roots.

## Conclusions

There has been a triple shift since 2014. First, Russia is much more aggressive towards all of its neighbours. But it is also more demanding of them. Despite economic pressures, Russia is not retrenching (Secrieru 2016); but it is looking for more value-for-money in all its relationships. The old subsidy regime cannot be as generous as it was, and, with Russia struggling to subsidise Crimea and the Donbas, it is pretty clear that it could not afford to pay all the bills of an extra nine and a half million Belarusians.

Second, Lukashenka has shifted in a more statist direction. Third, part of the old opposition has gone with him. But the biggest unknown is the things that may have changed the least. Public opinion in Belarus is shaped by Russian media and remains strongly Russophile. This is only changing slowly. The Belarusian public is also instrumental. There is support for paternalism from whatever source (IISEPS opinion polls do not directly address the question of whether Belarusians care who provides the welfare they undoubtedly value). There is only limited evidence that the population shares the elite's concerns about national security.

One lesson from eastern and southern Ukraine is that it is the moment of conflict that strengthens loyalty to the existing state. Pro-Ukrainian sentiment in the east and south has risen, but not because of the three months of the Maidan, largely because of the two years of war that followed. Belarus has not been invaded, but a sense of threat, and a desire to stay out of conflict, has led to a certain closing of ranks.

There is also some inertia in the system after twenty two years of Lukashenka. The sinews of the state are stronger than they were in Yanukovych's Ukraine. It would be much easier for Russia to impose their own guy at the top rather than break the bonds between the leader and the elite, or between the leader and society. So Belarus may have some strength in reserve.

---

[1]   Kimitaka Matsuzato, 'A Populist Island in an Ocean of Clan Politics: The Lukashenka Regime as an Exception Among CIS Countries', *Europe-Asia Studies,* vol. 56, no. 2, March 2004.

## References

Aliachnovič, Alieś, 2015. How Russia's Subsidies Save the Belarusian Economy, *Belarus Digest*, 26 August. Available at: <http://belarusdigest.com/story/how-russias-subsidies-save-belarusian-economy-23118>

Astapenia, Ryhor and Balkunets, Dzmitry, 2016. Belarus-Russia Relations after the Ukraine Conflict, *Ostrogorski Centre Analytical Paper*, no. 5, 1 August, p. 18. Available at: <http://belarusdigest.com/story/analytical-paper-belarus-russia-relations-after-ukraine-conflict-26617>

Balmaceda, Margarita, 2014a. Energy Policy in Belarus: Authoritarian Resilience, Social Contracts, and Patronage in a Post-Soviet Environment, *Eurasian Geography and Economics*, vol. 55, no. 5, pp. 514-36, p. 515.

Balmaceda, Margarita, 2014b. *Living the High Life in Minsk: Russian Energy Rents, Domestic Populism and Belarus' Impending Crisis.* Budapest: Central European University Press, p. 120.

Belarus Segodnia, 2015. For the Future of Independent Belarus!, 16 September. Available at: <www.sb.by/prezident-belarusi/article/za-budushchee-nezavisimoy-belarusi.html>

Bohdan, Siarhei and Astapenia, Ryhor, 2016. Why Belarus KGB Detained the Country's Former Top Businessman', *Belarus Digest*, 18 March. Available at: <http://belarusdigest.com/story/why-belarus-kgb-detained-countrys-former-top-businesman-25014>

Bohdan, Siarhei, 2015. Why Ukraine Failed to Revolutionize Belarus, *Belarus Digest*, 28 May. Available at: <http://belarusdigest.com/story/why-ukraine-failed-revolutionize-belarus-22802>

Coalson, Robert and Jozwiak, Rikard, 2015. Worried about Moscow, Belarus's Lukashenka Drifts toward Brussels, *RFE/RL*, 27 January. Available at: <www.rferl.org/a/belarus-lukashenka-drifts-toward-brussels/26816183.html>

Deutsche Welle, 2015. Lukashenko Dashes Hopes of Economic Reform at Inauguration, 6 November. Available at: <www.dw.com/en/lukashenko-dashes-hopes-of-economic-reform-at-inauguration/a-18833472>

Drakakhrust, Yury, 2016a. Whose Side Is Belarus on Anyway?, *Open Democracy*, 12 May. Available at: <www.opendemocracy.net/od-russia/yury-drakakhrust/whose-side-is-belarus-on-anyway>

Drakakhrust, Yury, 2016b. Public Opinion: Back to Reality, *Belarusian Yearbook 2016*. Available at: <http://nmnby.eu/yearbook/2016/en/page23.html>

Goble, Paul, 2016. Minsk Fears Moscow May Organize Hybrid War and Coloured Revolution in Belarus, *Eurasian Daily Monitor*, vol. 13, no. 116, 28 June. Available at: <https://jamestown.org/program/minsk-fears-moscow-may-organize-hybrid-war-and-color-revolution-in-belarus/>

IISEPS, 2014a. Vsesil'na li propaganda?, 5 July. Available at: <http://old.iiseps. org/06-14-08.html>

IISEPS, 2014b. Ukrainskii kompas dlia geopoliticheskikh poliusov Belarusi, September. Available at: <www.old.iiseps.org/09-14-04.html>

IISEPS, 2015a. Dislike for the Power Doesn't Transform into a Wish to Protest. Available at: <www.iiseps.org/?p=861&lang=en>

IISEPS, 2015b. The Most Important Results of the Public Opinion Poll in June 2015. Available at: <www.iiseps.org/?p=2678&lang=en>

IISEPS, 2015c. The Most Important Results of the Public Opinion Poll in December 2015, 29 December. Available at: <www.iiseps.org/?p=3865&lang=en>

IISEPS, 2015d. Khorosha Evropa, da ne pro nas. Available at: <www.old. iiseps.org/06-15-05.html>

Ioffe, Grigory and Yarashevich, Viachaslau, 2011. Debating Belarus: An Economy in Comparative Perspective, *Eurasian Geography and Economics*, vol. 52, no. 6.

Ioffe, Grigory, 2014. *Reassessing Lukashenka: Belarus in Cultural and Geopolitical Context.* Houndmills and New York: Palgrave Macmillan.

Karatch, Olga, 2016. Opinion: Four Russian Instruments of Control over Belarus, *Belarus Digest*, 13 September. Available at: <http://belarusdigest.com/story/opinion-four-russian-instruments-control-over-belarus-27210>

Liakhovich, Andrei, 2012. The Role of Security Services in Belarus Politics, *Belarus Digest*, 14 March. Available at: <http://belarusdigest.com/story/role-security-services-belarus-politics-8331>

Matsuzato, Kimitaka, 2004. A Populist Island in an Ocean of Clan Politics: The Lukashenka Regime as an Exception Among CIS Countries, *Europe-Asia Studies*, vol. 56, no. 2.

Minsk. Novosti, 2016. A. Lukashenko: Belarus' za gody nezavisimosti ne dala vtianut' sebia ni v odnu politicheskuiu avantiuru, 3 July. Available at: <http:// minsknews.by/blog/2016/07/03/a-lukashenko-belarus-za-godyi-nezavisimosti-ne-dala-vtyanut-sebya-ni-v-odnu-politicheskuyu-avantyuru/>

Mojeiko, Vadim, 2015a. Post-Maidan Belarus: Demand for Stability and More Belarusianness, *Bell*, no. 2. Available at: <www.eesc.lt/uploads/news/id849/Bell%20Nr.2_2015_.pdf>

Mojeiko, Vadim, 2015b. Soft Belarusization: a New Shift in Lukashenka's Domestic Policy?, *Belarus Digest*, 21 April. Available at: <http://belarusdigest.com/story/soft-belarusization-new-shift-lukashenkas-domestic-policy-22434>

Novaia gazeta, 2015. Lukashenko: Belorussiia ne chast' "russkogo mira", 29 January. Available at: <www.novayagazeta.ru/news/2015/01/29/109671-lukashenko-belorussiya-150-ne-chast-171-russkogo-mira-187>

Popov, Eduard, 2016. Popov: «Lukashenko Is Repeating Yanukovich's Mistakes», *Fort Russ*, 3 July. Available at: <www.fort-russ.com/2016/07/popov-lukashenko-is-repeating.html>

Pranevičiūtė-Neliupšienė, J. and Maksimiuk, Z., 2014. Authoritarian Bargain in Belarus: The System of Social Benefits as a Factor of Regime Stability, in Pranevičiūtė-Neliupšienė et al eds., *Belarusian Regime Longevity: Happily Ever After.* Vilnius: Vilnius University Publishing House, pp. 124-156.

Rettman, Andrew, 2016. West Told Ukraine to Abandon Crimea, Document Says, *EU Observer*, 24 February. Available at: <https://euobserver.com/foreign/132425>

Rutkowski, Bartosz, Rychły, Marcin and Zaniewicz, Maciej, 2016. The Complicated Story of the Belarusian Opposition, *New Eastern Europe*, no. 1 (January-February), pp. 131-137.

Secrieru, Stanislav, 2016. Why Russia Does not Retrench, *New Eastern Europe*, no. 5.

Shraibman, Artyom, 2015. What Makes the 2015 Belarus Presidential Campaign So Different?, *Belarus Digest,* 4 August. Available at: <http://belarusdigest.com/story/what-makes-2015-belarus-presidential-campaign-so-different-22989>

Simmons, Katie, Stokes, Bruce and Poushter, Jacob, 2015. Ukrainian Public Opinion: Dissatisfied with Current Conditions, Looking for an End to the Crisis, *Pew Research Center*, 10 June. Available at: <www.pewglobal.org/2015/06/10/3-ukrainian-public-opinion-dissatisfied-with-current-conditions-looking-for-an-end-to-the-crisis/>

Smok, Vadzim, 2014. New Polls: Belarusians Support Lukashenka and Do Not Want an Euromaidan, *Belarus Digest*, 2 May. Available at: <http://belarusdigest.com/story/new-polls-belarusians-support-lukashenka-and-do-not-want-euromaidan-17707>

Tut.by, 2015. BPF Is Calling to Drop the Maidan Idea and Nominate Kastusiou for Presidency, 7 March. Available at: <http://news.tut.by/politics/438685.html>

Tynchenko, Yaroslav, 2015. Muscle Flexing in the North', *Ukrainian Week*, no. 4 (April), pp. 40-43. Available at: <http://i.tyzhden.ua/content/photoalbum/2015/04_2015/27/Book4.pdf>

Way, Lucan, 2015. *Pluralism by Default: Weak Autocrats and the Rise of Competitive Politics*. Baltimore: John Hopkins University Press.

Website of the President of Belarus, 2016. Belarus President's Speech at the Independence Day Military Parade, 3 July. Available at: <http://president.gov.by/en/news_en/view/belarus-presidents-speech-at-the-independence-day-military-parade-13963/>

White, Stephen and Feklyunina, Valentina, 2014. *Identities and Foreign Policies in Russia, Ukraine and Belarus: the Other Europes.* Basingstoke and New York: Palgrave Macmillan.

Yarashevich, Viachaslau, 2014. Political Economy of Modern Belarus: Going against Mainstream? *Europe-Asia Studies*, vol. 66, no.10, pp. 1703-1734.

Yeliseyeu, Andrei, 2014. Protest Activity in Ukraine and Belarus and Belarusian Public Attitude towards Maidan, *Bell*, no. 2. Available at: <www.eesc.lt/uploads/news/id728/Bell%202014%202%20(44).pdf>

# Belarus–China Relations

## BY
## PETER BRAGA

**Jelisiejeŭ, A.**
Some Aspects of Belarusian-Chinese Relations
in the Regional Dimension: Much Sound and Little Sense.
The Belarusian Institute for Strategic Studies: Minsk, 2013, 22 pp.
Report No. SA #08/2013RU.

**Šrajbman, A.**
Belorussko-kitaiskie otnosheniia: ozhidaniia, problemy i perspektivy.
Friedrich Ebert Stiftung Foundation: Kyiv, 2014, 11 pp.
Report No. 2014.

**Jakoŭčyk, K.**
The Good, the Bad, and the Ambitious:
Democracy and Autocracy Promoters Competing in Belarus.
European Political Science Review, 2015, 30 pp.
DOI:10.1017/S1755773914000459.

According to the official narrative in Minsk, Belarus–China relations have been one long success story of fast-rising trade figures and ever larger Chinese investments. Among independent analysts, however, there is unease over the relationship. Critics worry that Belarus is sacrificing precious state funds on costly joint projects with little to show for it. Three recent articles–when taken together– explain the nature of Belarus–China relations and rectify the disparities between the conflicting official and independent narratives.

The three articles make two things clear about Belarus–China relations: (1) the regime's drive to bring in Chinese investment has committed it to a high-risk strategy; (2) if cooperation continues to deepen, there will be political and economic implications for China, the EU, Belarus and the surrounding region.

The first article, written by Andrej Jelisiejeŭ, offers an insightful and candid narrative of the development of China–Belarus relations. The second is a fascinating piece by Arciom Šrajbman. It inspects micro-level details on China's foreign direct investment (FDI) in Belarus. The third, by Kaciaryna Jakoŭčyk, is extremely useful, because it considers the Belarus–China relationship within a wider, geopolitical context. Together, the three articles compliment each another – moving first from a general, then to a detailed, and finally to a global perspective.

Belarus–China relations have only really begun to develop in the last decade. Leading into 2006, it became apparent that Russian companies would soon stop transiting natural gas through Belarus at subsidised rates. Belarus had been able to capitalise on this arrangement by selling gas onward to Europe at world market prices. The Belarusian authorities were about to lose a substantial source of revenue. Deepening economic cooperation with China was seen as a possible solution.

Starting in 2006, Andrej Jelisiejeŭ, an analyst with the Belarusian Institute for Strategic Studies, summarises the development of relations with a critical eye. For Jelisiejeŭ, the issues lie in what gets overlooked or misinterpreted. He sees a disconnect between official rhetoric and the reality on the ground. In particular, Jelisiejeŭ demonstrates that Belarus is neither a unique nor a favoured partner of China's. He accomplishes this by first defining the levels of importance China applies to its foreign partnerships. Then, he shows that Belarus did not receive the highest status of relations with China – a 'strategic partnership' – until 2013, years behind Ukraine, Poland and Russia. He also shows that Belarusian officials seem to have been wholly unaware of China's hierarchy of foreign partnerships. Neither are fast rising trade figures exclusive to Belarus–China relations. Belarus shares comparable, if not lower trade growth statistics with neighbouring East European states.

Jelisiejeŭ uses several revealing quotes from a trove of diplomatic cables published on Wikileaks to argue that China is hesitant, if not entirely uninterested in Belarus as an investment destination. 'The Soviet economic mind-set remains, and Belarusian technology that may have been of interest ten years ago has deteriorated, while Chinese standards and demands have risen,' a former Chinese Ambassador is quoted to have said (Jelisiejeŭ, p. 15). Beyond specialised potash fertilisers, the author argues, Belarus can only offer China its political support (taking China's position on UN resolutions for example). In comparison to EU member states, such as Poland, Belarus is a poor 'gateway' for Chinese trade to Europe, cautions Jelisiejeŭ. He concludes that Belarus–China relations are more hype than substance.

To some readers, Jelisiejeŭ may appear overly negative. Perhaps there may come a day when 'Belarus will hardly interest China with enough promising projects to disburse the entire amount [of loans China has put forward]' (Jelisiejeŭ,

p. 16). In the meantime, however, China continues to extend new lines of credit, and Belarus would be hard pressed to find better borrowing terms elsewhere. At the same time, his negativity is refreshing (and perhaps needed); it helps to shake off the stupor of Minsk's seemingly blind optimism.

Jelisiejeŭ's study provides a strong foundation to evaluate bilateral ties as they continue to develop. However, it does have one (forgivable) deficiency: timing. Months after the publication of Jelisiejeŭ's paper, President Xi Jinping announced China's ambitious 'One Belt, One Road' infrastructure project (often referred to as the Silk Road project). Since then, the argument for Belarus to act as a Chinese manufacturing and logistics hub on Europe's eastern doorstep has gained greater momentum.

The One Belt, One Road (OBOR) project is an ambitious plan to expand rail links from China to Europe and coordinate them with seaports and maritime trade (reminiscent of the ancient Silk Road). The oddly named 'One Road' component consists of ports and shipping facilities to increase seaborne trade from East Asia, which in turn are supposed to integrate with the railways of the 'One Belt' to move goods overland, rather than crossing two oceans along the current route. Belarusian officials claim that Belarus is a perfectly placed 'gateway' for Central Asian and Russian railways from China to merge before entering Europe.

Arciom Šrajbman, a political commentator for the online news portal TUT. BY, has the benefit of writing a year following the announcement of the OBOR. Šrajbman targets a similar audience to Jelisiejeŭ – foreign observers and Belarusian analysts – and scrutinises China's foreign aid and joint projects in Belarus. He pays particular attention to Belarus's 'springboard' for the OBOR into Europe – the Great Stone Industrial Park (GSIP). The GSIP is a massive manufacturing and logistics joint development lying southeast of Minsk. It is modelled on the China–Singapore Suzhou Industrial Park, and is intended to handle incoming freight from the OBOR.

Unlike Jelisiejeŭ, who sees relations as being essentially dead in the water, Šrajbman understands that Belarus–China relations are still evolving. However, it becomes clear the Belarusian strategy to attract Chinese investment involves a great deal of risk. Šrajbman reveals that while China may offer loans free of political conditionality (no requirements to hold democratic elections, release political prisoners, promote freedom of the press, or reduce state involvement in the economy), it attaches commercial conditionality (explained below) to ensure its own economic benefit.

For Šrajbman, a core problem for the Belarus–China relationship is the expectation that Belarus intends to gain more from China, rather than the other way around. This expectation permeates all two-way interactions. The result is that bilateral relations can be summarised as Belarusian enthusiasm and Chinese caution.

In order to hedge against its concerns, Beijing takes measures to ensure the credit it doles out turns a profit. These measures are commercial conditions that govern when and how its loans can be used. For example, 50 percent (and sometimes 70 percent) of Chinese credit to Belarus must come in the form of Chinese sourced goods, equipment and services. In effect, China is ensuring both its investment in the Belarusian economy and export of its own finished products.

With reference to several existing joint projects, Šrajbman illustrates that China's calculating approach confronts Belarus with three problems. First, commercial conditionality means that Chinese credit is essentially tied up until Belarus can satisfy Chinese requirements. For example, Belarus has already invested 'a great deal of money in the [GSIP],' but the Chinese side is holding back on its side of the investment until Belarus satisfies more conditions (Šrajbman, p. 8). Second, stipulations that it must buy finished Chinese industrial goods restricts how Belarus can spend what it borrows. Third, it loses control over its suppliers, and must rely on quality decisions from the Chinese side. In their effort to bring in Chinese investment, Belarusian officials have unwittingly placed their country in a somewhat compromised position.

What Šrajbman does not do is convincingly explain why Minsk is willing to take these risks. He notes that Belarusian officials wish to break the tiring dichotomy of playing the EU off against Russia for external support. However, beyond acknowledging this fact, Šrajbman does not elaborate on the rationale for using China as a third, great power partner to balance Belarus's foreign relations. Neither does he discuss the wider, geopolitical implications of China's growing presence and influence in Belarus. This is what Jakoŭčyk's study provides.

Kaciaryna Jakoŭčyk, Jean Monnet Chair for European Politics at the University of Passau, Germany, places China's growing presence in Belarus into geopolitical context. She details the strong external influences major powers have upon Belarus, which the other two authors only refer to in passing.

Jakoŭčyk views the Belarus–China relationship under the lens of democracy and autocracy promotion. This approach focuses on how states use foreign policy instruments to promote the spread of democratic or authoritarian political systems. The system in Belarus is electoral authoritarianism. Despite having elections, political pluralism is limited and checks on power are subverted to suit the incumbent regime. The EU, Russia and China act as either democracy or autocracy promoters.

In her theoretical framework, Jakoŭčyk systematizes the competition between promoters. The EU – via its Eastern Partnership initiative – is an active democracy promoter. Russia uses a range of foreign policy tools to actively promote autocracy. She argues that China, on the other hand, is a *passive* autocracy promoter. Unlike the EU or Russia, China is committed to a noninterventionist foreign policy and politics-free deal making. Therefore, China does not deliberately spread autocracy. Rather, it either indirectly competes for or complements the spread of authoritarian rule.

Lying between the EU and Russia, Belarus is a geopolitical battle ground within a larger global struggle of democracy versus autocracy. She argues the Belarus–China relationship could both prolong undemocratic rule in Belarus and enable China – a potential future authoritarian great power rival – to establish a presence along the EU's eastern borders.

For Belarus, the ideal geopolitical relationship is for China to act as a stabiliser, which will allow Minsk to balance its linkages (cultural, diplomatic, economic and military ties) with Russia and the EU. In this scenario, China represents strings-free economic support, because of its non-intervention foreign policy and willingness to engage without political conditionality. This 'is convenient for Belarus, which does not plan to voluntarily conduct any political liberalisation that might threaten the current regime' (Jakoŭčyk, p. 19).

However, at times Jakoŭčyk almost seems carried away by her own narrative. She characterises Chinese policy towards Belarus as a 'charm offensive,' which is the approach China took with Central Asian regimes (Jakoŭčyk, p. 13–14). The development of Belarus–China ties is different to that of Central Asia. As Jelisiejeŭ shows, Belarus has been the one constantly trying to woo China, not the other way around.

There are other deficiencies. In figure 4 and table 1, she compares sources of FDI and loans to Belarus. However, she does not explore the structure or effectiveness of the investments and aid. It is important to do so because as Šrajbman shows, commercial conditionality can, in fact, have political implications. For example, the stalling of a joint project, such as the GSIP, due to nonfulfillment of commercial conditionality will reflect poorly on the regime's image of legitimacy and competence in guiding the economy.

Lastly, Jakoŭčyk's definition of China as a passive autocracy promoter is ambiguous. China apparently competes for or complements the promotion of autocracy. At the same time, 'China does not have any intention to export to Belarus any model of a particular form of rule or to shape its political system' (Jakoŭčyk, p. 23).

The problem is that Jakoŭčyk's theoretical model is too one-dimensional: Belarus must be given greater agency. Perspective must be shifted from the autocratic patron (China) to the illiberal client (Belarus). The Belarusian regime seeks support from China to prolong its own survival and continue authoritarian rule. Therefore, China neither actively nor passively promotes, and is better understood as a patron. As Jakoŭčyk herself notes, China does not intend to promote any kind of autocracy in Belarus, but '[n]evertheless, China is supporting the Belarusian regime' (Jakoŭčyk, p. 23).

Despite all the potential pitfalls, Belarus–China relations continue to develop. China's presence in Belarus and its influence in Eastern Europe continues to grow. In their desperation to bring in Chinese investment, however, policy makers have locked Belarus into costly joint projects with reduced bargaining power. In many ways, China has not been the escape from EU and Russian cross-conditionality the Belarusian regime was hoping for.

The three articles reviewed here get to the heart of Belarus–China relations. Jelisiejeŭ produces an excellent overview of the development of bilateral ties. Šrajbman complements this with a fascinating analysis of joint projects in Belarus. Jakoŭčyk provides a much needed discussion on China–Belarus relations at the level of geopolitics, although at times she fails to take important realities into account.

Future studies need to consider regional developments, such as Russia's economic slowdown, Western sanctions, the 2014 Ukraine crisis and, in due course, Brexit. All these events will likely have an effect on the Belarus–China relationship. Other studies that focus more directly on bilateral ties between China and Belarus must account for the continued development of the OBOR infrastructure project. In addition, Jelisiejeŭ only briefly touches on Belarusian FDI (or lack thereof) to China. A more detailed study on the subject is needed.

The three papers reviewed here may be a year or so behind current events. Nevertheless, the hierarchy of Chinese diplomatic relations cited by Jelisiejeŭ, the detail on Chinese commercial conditionality provided by Šrajbman, and the geopolitical context modelled by Jakoŭčyk make these studies essential for properly understanding the nature of Belarus–China relations.

# Awaking in One's Own Country

## BY

## DŹMITRY PAPKO

**Valancin Akudovič**
Awaking in One's Own Country, Łohvinaŭ: Vilnius, 2015. 286 pages.
20 BYN
ISBN: 9786098147476

*Awaking in One's Own Country* is a new collection of texts written by Valancin Akudovič, a renowned Belarusian philosopher. Akudovič sets out to prove that language, history, and culture are not after all so important in the nation-building process – the process of constructing the nation's collective identification as Belarusian. Instead, the most important factor is merely the fact that a country or state exists. This exerts a more tangible influence on people's everyday lives. When Belarusians take money out of their pocket – they see Belarusian money. When they join the army, they join the Belarusian army, and when they go to gaol – they are put in a Belarusian gaol and not sent to Siberia. Moreover, they have their own president, their own television channels, and, what's more, they even have their own dictator at the very top of the state. All of this makes Belarusians become more Belarusian every day, little by little.

Valancin Akudovič remains probably the most famous Belarusian philosopher. A graduate of the Gorky Literary Institute (Moscow, 1980), Akudovič went on to work in the weeklies *Kultura* and *LiM* and the magazines *Krynica* and *Frahmienty.* Akudovič's works have been translated into Swedish, Polish, Russian, and Lithuanian.

Writing about the national cultural canon, Valancin Akudovič aptly points out that there was only a 15-year gap between the 'Spring of Nations' in 1848, which marked the beginning of many European nationalisms, and the Kalinoŭski uprising , which signalled the beginning of a Belarusian national movement. In other words, in the context of the era of nationalism, the Belarusians experienced a 'national awakening' at more or less the same time as many other European nations. However, the comprehensive search for a particularly Belarusian idea began only after the end of the Russian revolution of 1905. The Vilnia newspaper *Naša Niva*, alongside the cultural and political milieus which emerged under its influence, played a crucial role in the Belarusian movement. At this time, most of the national cultural canon was established, and it lasted until the end of the 20th century without major transformations.

Akudovič provides a careful analysis of a number of important aspects of the Belarusian state: the geopolitical (Belarus in its ethnographic borders), cultural (domination of the Belarusian language and culture), historical (continuity with the Principality of Połack and the Great Duchy of Lithuania), political (national democracy) and, finally, constitutional (an independent state).

*Awaking in One's Own Country* is also an important book for the history of Belarusian philosophy. Akudovič suggests that the 1990s constituted the most significant period in the history of Belarusian thinking as such, as this was the first time it had manifested itself clearly and systematically in this role. The philosopher mentions what he believes to be two of the most iconic projects of that era – the literary-philosophical fascicle ZNO in the weekly *Kultura* (1993-1997), and the first truly Belarusian philosophical magazine *Frahmienty* (1996), which represented the most vivid manifestation of the collective intervention of Belarusians into the philosophical space. Akudovič notes that the most remarkable feature of these projects was their aspiration to isolate the discourse surrounding the universal entirety of Belarusian culture and to record it independently as just one (extremely significant) dimension of this culture.

In his book, Valancin Akudovič provides a thorough bibliography, often citing works of thinkers such as Heidegger, Junger, José Ortega y Gasset, and Sloterdijk. However, Akudovič often refers to works written by other Belarusians. In particular, the author regrets the fact that studies of different iterations of the Belarusian national idea have often disregarded the extent to which these concepts are intertwined, a brilliant example of which being an essay by Ihnat Abdzirałovič (Kančeŭski) entitled 'On the Eternal Way'.

Akudovič emphasises that Ihnat Abdzirałovič was the first Belarusian to renounce a Belarusian national idea, suggesting in its place the concept of an 'eternal Belarusian way'. In another projection, instead of the idea as a logocentric form, he popularised the concept of the 'streaming form', resembling Foucault's notion of 'discourse'.

The book also contains the author's reflections on the state of modern philosophy. Akudovič notes that philosophy is rapidly being marginalized. According to him, as with literature, philosophy began voluntarily renouncing the 'heights' (of metaphysics) in favour of a mutual understanding of the contexts of the 'surface,' the permanent domain of the everyman. However, unlike in literature, where this 'fall' occurred by means of a simplification of language and a paradigm shift away from literature as a heuristic, philosophy (which cannot by definition follow this course) firstly stopped being concerned with its 'highest discourse' – metaphysics, and then reformatted itself to suit social and political sciences.

The author argues that philosophy has no prospects today as a discipline. 'Disciplinary' philosophers will move further towards what is sometimes called 'social thinking' or simply move on to fields in which analytical or reflective skills are required. Philosophy is becoming even more thoroughly embedded in aesthetic discourses, especially in literature. Fiction has been moving towards non-fiction (real history) and philosophy has been moving towards fiction (reflective literature). Philosophy – as we understand the term today – will gradually return to its pre-institutional roots, the era of 'schools' and 'academies' of antiquity, when individuals opened practices to engage in philosophy.

The book also contains the author's reflections on various other subjects.

Akudovič touches upon the problem of Čarnobyl as compared with previous tragedies faced by Belarusians, including the many endless and merciless wars which were perpetually fought in the Belarusian lands. The author points out that the Čarnobyl disaster was not the most significant catastrophe for the nation in terms of scale: As in the case of wars and occupations, people had to put out fires, leave their homes, die from 'cholera', mourn their dead and worry about their children's future.

Later, the philosopher brilliantly describes the fate of Mark Chagall in the context of Belarus. Akudovič describes how the 'Belarusian factor' gradually became an important element for Chagall's work and, in a certain way, perhaps the primary theme, as the Belarusian space (Viciebsk) provided Chagall with an existential place in life. Moreover, if we consider this existentiality not only in the context of temporal time but also in the domain of personal space, we can recognize Chagall the Jew also as a Belarusian, accepting that it is fully legitimate to characterize him as possessing 'dual nationality'.

Valancin Akudovič also goes on to offer advice to the Nobel Committee regarding prize-worthy modern Belarusian writers. According to him, Aleś Razanaŭ is the Belarusian most worthy of the Nobel Prize. Akudovič explains his choice by arguing that a winner of the world's most prestigious literary award must be open to the possibility of discovering new senses and contents of human existence or non-existence in literature.

The book is written in simple language, so despite the seriousness of the material, it is very readable. The author masterfully uses rich vocabulary, even if questions sometimes arise regarding word choice. For example, in some situations the author uses calques from other Slavic languages when accurate Belarusian equivalents are available.

*Awaking in One's Own Country* is a book that has great cultural significance for Belarusian philosophy. Moreover, Valancin Akudovič's book occupies an important place in the social and political discourse. Impressively, Akudovič manages to remain a 'neutral analyst' despite his participation in numerous events described in the book, which are illustrated by numerous personal anecdotes. He masterfully offers his reader a look at well-known events seen from a different angle and placed in a larger perspective.

———————————

# Annual Report of the Chairman of the Anglo-Belarusian Society for 2015

BY

BRIAN BENNETT

2015 was a busy year for the Society. As well as the usual events of Mother Language Day, Kupallie, Kaliady and Batliejka, we organised an event in memory of Guy Picarda, a lecture by Dr Suša of the Belarusian National Library and presentations on Belarusian Nobel Prize winners. We supported a UCL conference on Grand Duchy micro-histories, the annual UCL Belarus lecture given by Per Rudling, and a book launch by Prof Arnold McMillin. We also said farewell to Fr Alexander and Count Ciechanowiecki both, in very different ways, staunch supporters of the Society. We were happy to see the Skaryna Library open to the public and construction begin on a new wooden church in the grounds of Marian House.

The year began as usual with the Annual General Meeting in Marian House on **24 January.** We heard reports from Society post-holders, elected a new Council and reviewed the past year. Among the issues discussed were ways to increase the number of formal members of the Society so as to put the management and finances of the society on a sounder footing, but what emerged was a continuing preference for the present informal 'pay-as-you-go' arrangements. The meeting agreed to protest the treatment of the Minsk bookshop Lohvinau and, in a joint action with the Skaryna Library in London, I duly wrote to the Belarusian Ambassador in London on 27 January to express the Society's deep concern at the heavy fine imposed on it.

Mother Language Day was held on **21 February** in Marian House. Organised jointly with St Cyril's Sunday School, it was very well attended with a lot of audience participation and enjoyment.

UCL organised a conference on Grand Duchy of Lithuania micro histories **20-21 March** at SSEES. The Society's Patron was among those supporting it. The keynote speaker was Prof David Crick and papers were presented by historians from Belarus, Lithuania, Poland, the UK and the USA.

The well-attended Annual London Lecture on Belarusian Studies, organised by the UCL and the Ostrogorski Centre with the support of the Association of

Belarusians in Great Britain, was given by Professor Per Anders Rudling at SEES on **25 March** in cooperation with the Society and others.

Fr Alexander Nadson, head of the Belarusian Catholic Mission in the UK since 1959, passed away on **15 April** and was laid to rest in the Islington and St Pancras Cemetery on **29 April** after a Uniate service in St Mary's Roman Catholic Church just opposite. Amongst his many activities he had been Chairman and Vice-President of the Society and librarian of the Belarusian Library and Museum in London (the Skaryna Library). I represented the Society at his funeral, attended by many other members. He was a unique man with a unique history; we shall not see his like again.

On **13 June** we held an event in memory of Guy Picarda, attended by his daughters Alice and Eloise. He had been Chairman of the Society and a major figure in the diaspora supporting Belarusian culture. Jim Dingley gave a talk on his life and the D L Singers sang Belarusian part songs from a collection Guy had brought together in 'Bielaruś Zalataja'.

We were pleased to see our friend and neighbour, the important Skaryna Library in Holden Road, open for visitors and students in June.

After Kupallie on **DATE** and the summer break we gathered at Marian House on **17 October** for a lecture by Dr Alies Suša of the Belarusian National Library.

The Society was represented at the funeral on **16 November** of Count Andrzej Ciechanowiecki, a major figure in the art world and patron of historical cultural restoration in Belarus. He was Patron of the Society.

On **21 November** there was an event at Marian House consisting of presentations on Belarusian Nobel Prize winners and nominees, particularly Svetlana Alexievich who had just been awarded the Nobel Prize for Literature.

Prof Arnold McMillin, Vice President of the Society, launched his book 'Spring Shoots: Young Belarusian Poets in the Early Twenty-First Century' at UCL on **26 November**.

The end of year Christmas festivities were marked at Marian House by a Nativity Play on **19 December** organised by the Belarusian Sunday School led by headmistress Natallia Ramančuk, and Kaliady and Batliejka on **24 December**.

# Authors of Articles and Book Reviews

PETER BRAGA, PhD candidate, School of Slavonic and East European Studies, University College London, peter.braga.15@ucl.ac.uk

VERANIKA LAPUTSKA, PhD candidate, Graduate School for Social Research, Institute of Philosophy and Sociology, Polish Academy of Sciences, veranika.laputska@east-center.org

DŹMITRY PAPKO, PhD candidate, University of Warsaw, vinsentmusic@gmail.com

ALEKSANDRA POMIECKO, PhD candidate, Department of History, University of Toronto, aleks.pomiecko@mail.utoronto.ca

INA SHAKHRAI, PhD candidate, Department of Social Sciences, Humboldt University of Berlin, ina.shakhrai@gmail.com

ANDREW WILSON, Professor in Ukrainian Studies, University College London, tjmsalw@ucl.ac.uk

www.ingramcontent.com/pod-product-compliance
Lightning Source LLC
Chambersburg PA
CBHW060422290526
45791CB00002B/848